Wisdom With Understanding is Better Than Rubies

Laurine Karon Greenberg
Fine Arts Collection

Mystic Chords

Mystic Chords

Mysticism and Psychology in Popular Music

Manish Soni

Algora Publishing
New York

Algora Publishing, New York
© 2001 by Algora Publishing
All rights reserved. Published 2001.
Printed in the United States of America
ISBN: 1-892941-71-6
Editors@algora.com

Library of Congress Cataloging-in-Publication Data 2001-004694

Soni, Manish.
Mystic chords : mysticism and psychology in popular music / by Manish
Soni.
    p. cm.
ISBN 1-892941-71-6 (alk. paper)
1. Rock music—Religious aspects. 2. Rock music—Psychological
aspects. 3. Mysticism. I. Title.
ML3918.R63 S66 2001
781.64'11—dc21
                                2001004694

Cover photos
Pompey Fresco

New York
www.algora.com

To my wife, Kirti, for her infinite patience while I worked on this book, and to my daughter, Malavika, for being a living inspiration

Contents

Introduction   3

PART ONE — Mysticism   9

Chapter 1: The Spirit of Mysticism   ·   11
    Mysticism versus Religion, — 12. The Mystical Life, — 17.
    Detachment, Renunciation, Wu-Wei, — 21.

Chapter 2: The Nature of the World and the Self   29
    The World as Illusion, — 29. Form and Matter, — 32. The
    Unity of all Consciousness, 36. Time and Change, — 40.

Chapter 3: Awakening of the True Self   47
    Realization of the Great Unity, — 47. The Higher Dimen-
    sion, — 50. Love as Mystical Union, — 57. The Roots of Dis-
    cord, — 60. Transforming Perception, — 62. Kundalini —
    Ascent of the Serpent Power, — 69.

Chapter 4: The Mystical Perspective   79
    The Original State of Mind, — 79. Emergence of Ego and
    Consciousness, — 82. Unity of Opposites, — 85. The Web of
    Life/Gaia Theory, — 87. Reincarnation and Karma, — 91. Ego
    Dissolution and The Great Void, — 95.

1

PART TWO — Psychology   101

Chapter 5: Psychology and Mysticism   103
    The Similarities, — 103. The Differences, — 106. The Nature
    of the Unconscious, — 108. Imbalance and Compensation, —
    110.

Chapter 6: Mind, World and Projection   115
    The Mind and Its Productions, — 115. Archetypes and the
    Collective Unconscious, — 121. Childhood Psyche, — 126.
    Psychoanalysis and Childhood, — 128.

Chapter 7: Society and the Individual   139
    The Nature and Function of Society, — 140. Society and
    Ego, — 147. To Thine Own Self Be True, — 149. Society and
    Sanity, — 152. From Nurture to Nihilism, — 154.

Chapter 8: Expansion of Consciousness   167
    The Infinite Mind, — 167. The Destructive Unconscious, —
    169. Mystic and Hallucinatory Visions, — 173. The Use and
    Effects of Psychedelics, — 176. Drug Abuse and Psychic In-
    flation — The Velvet Underground's Heroin, 184.

PART THREE — The Hero Journey   193

Chapter 9: The Call to Adventure   195
    The Inward Journey, — 195. Discontentment and Separa-
    tion, — 199. Descent into the Deep, — 202.

Chapter 10: The Struggle and the Return   207
    The Mother Archetype, — 209. Bob Dylan's Isis, — 212. Re-
    turn to the Worldly Plane, — 217.

Conclusion   225
Appendix   237

Introduction

Rock and roll, and archetypal symbolism? If it is true that the creative spark of artistic inspiration originates deep within the collective
soul of humanity, then it must also be true that it encompasses all
forms of artistic expression and is not confined to any specific age or art
form. The same primal source from which mythology, dreams, folk traditions, and poetic insight arise must also be the inspirational source
for painting, music, literature, and all other modes of creative human
endeavor. Elitists may dismiss popular entertainment as not properly
belonging to this sphere of creative expression, but modern genres such
as rock music and movie-making deserve their rightful places alongside
the recognized works of classical and traditional art forms.

Much of popular music undoubtedly was produced for commercial
profit rather than as a means of true expression, but a great number of
the genuine pioneers of rock and roll did perceive music as a means of
connecting with the mystical source of energy and creation that lay
within their beings. The correspondence between the ideas and psychic
forces which find release through rock and roll and the symbolism of
religious, philosophical, and mythological imagery lends credence to
the proposition that all of these methods of assimilating, synthesizing,

and expressing archetypal psychological elements have a common origin deep within the human mind. It is that correspondence that forms the subject matter of this book.

Universal forces are at play within every individual and culture, but it is not possible to express them in their pristine and unmodified splendor, for they exist in a plane that conscious human thoughts and language simply cannot hope to attain. Therefore, when they do appear in the vastly limited world of which men are consciously aware, they are always clothed in the customs, images, and stylizations of the local culture and environment. The universal form lies concealed behind the local, temporal form. This local form may then either be believed in, religiously, or understood as a stepping stone — an interface through which the higher truth underlying it can be obtained.

When a series of highly profound and complex psychic factors (factors that greatly transcend the ordinary world of thoughts and senses) struggles to break through and make itself known to consciousness, it soon arrives at an impenetrable wall: the limitations of the human mind. The only way to reach the other side of this wall is through a tiny crack that appears there, the entry into the sentient and intellectual sphere of human apprehension. These great and transpersonal energies must constellate together into a sufficiently compressed mass so that they can make their way through the narrow fissure, and only then do they appear to man, unrecognizably altered and inextricably tangled together.

These energies now take the forms of symbols and abstract metaphors, and those who promulgate them are regarded as saviors, prophets, and visionaries, and are revered above all others. Receiving and correctly interpreting these highly charged, inestimably precious symbols is not within the power of the average man, and only those endowed with exceptional gifts for this crucial task can correctly understand them and elucidate their hidden significance. Carl Jung, the great psychologist, who did possess such a gift for symbolic interpretation, explained the nature of symbols thus:

> The word *symbol* comes from the Greek word *symballein*, to throw together. It has to do, then, with things gathered together, or with a heap of material thrown together, which we, as the expression shows,

take as a whole. We could translate the word symbol as "something viewed as a totality," or as "the vision of things brought into a whole." We must always have recourse to a symbol when we are dealing with a great variety of aspects or with a multiplicity of things which form a connected unit and which are so closely woven together in all their separate parts that we cannot separate or take away any parts without destroying the connections and losing the meaning of the totality. Modern philosophy has formulated this way of looking at things as *Gestalt* theory. A symbol, then, is a living *Gestalt*, or form — the sum total of a highly complex set of facts which our intellect cannot master conceptually, and which therefore cannot be expressed in any way other than by the use of an image.[1]

It is crucial that the symbols and images in any given culture match outer realities and fulfill inner needs within that specific cultural form; otherwise they lose their relevance and their meaning is perverted. A large factor in the spiritual and psychical problems of the current age is that most people still hold onto the symbols that were employed thousands of years ago, and there has been no attempt to understand the symbolic forms of *contemporary* self-expression, which are more attuned to the historico-cultural situation and circumstances of the present day. Inner realities are eternal and unchanging, but the symbols expressing them need to be constantly reinvented and reinterpreted, such that they are pertinent to the times and comprehensible to the people living in them. As Joseph Campbell writes:

All the life-potentialities that we never managed to bring to adult realization, those other portions of ourselves, are there [within us]; for such golden seeds do not die. If only a portion of that lost totality could be dredged up into the light of day, we should experience a marvelous expansion of our powers, a vivid renewal of life. We should tower in stature. Moreover, if we could dredge up something forgotten not only by ourselves but by our whole generation or our entire civilization, we should become indeed the boon-bringer, the culture hero of the day — a personage of not only local but world historical moment.[2]

There is no reason that one should search for such worldwide historical personages only in the annals of ancient history, in an age remote from us not only by eons but also by a vast gulf in mentality and outlook. In this age of technological advances and of human destruction on a scale previously unimaginable, a writer or artist who rediscovers the forgotten truths, yet who also takes into account current external realities, would speak far more directly to the people than a saint or prophet from the dim past who was trying to rectify the errors and misconceptions peculiar to *his* generation.

The Truth may be ever the same, but there are as many misapprehensions of it as there are different cultures and societies, and each one of them needs its "re-adjusters" to hold up a mirror to its prevalent delusions. The more the constituent symbols of the psyche are unearthed, see the light of day, and are properly comprehended, the less they remain unconscious, and hence awareness and clarity increase proportionally. Psychoanalysis has shown us that unconscious forces and motivations are in large part to blame for the maladies and conflicts that plague the world today. Modern songwriters, if they appreciate the significance of their role, can serve as such re-adjusters of mass consciousness, and thus they are charged with a serious responsibility. It was in recognition of this that Bob Dylan said:

> I'm a poet
> And I know it
> Hope I don't blow it.[3]

A number of artists having a well-publicized association with spiritual quests, Eastern philosophy, yoga, etc., are not mentioned in this book. Their omission might seem a little odd, at first; however, those who adopt mystical or occult elements from established philosophical or psychological traditions and transplant them essentially unaltered into their music are not of interest here. The focus is on original and pioneering thought in popular music that is paralleled and confirmed by visionaries from other disciplines who have ventured into the depths of the mind and unearthed some of its enduring mysteries. What I have attempted, here, is to draw together the fields of mysticism, philosophy, psychology, and literature with the seemingly disparate realm of popular music and culture,[4] and to achieve a cohesive synthesis of these.

Most people at some time in their lives question the nature of existence, and consciousness, but are usually met with bewildering paradoxes and suffer such setbacks in their quest that the task seems tantamount to the labors of Sisyphus. The lyrics by the rock group Queen, below, crystallize the essence of such existential soul-searching:

Is this the real life?
Is this just fantasy?
Caught in a landslide
No escape from reality
Open your eyes
Look up to the skies and see.[5]

There can be no doubt that many artists of the modern era, in their respective fields, have grappled with the same philosophical and metaphysical problems that have occupied the minds of thinking men and women throughout history. The reflective introspection voiced by Bob Dylan is perhaps as old as mankind itself, and in one way or another it has been the unceasing effort of every age to find some sort of meaningful resolution to these basic, unanswered questions:

Just like you
I'm wondering what I'm doing here
Just like you
I'm wondering what's going on.[6]

Footnotes

1. C. G. Jung, *The Psychology of Kundalini Yoga: Notes of the seminar given in 1932 by C. G. Jung.* The writings of Carl Jung are an especially bountiful source of insight in the context of this book, for he was one of the founders of Western psychology (specifically, analytical psychology) and at the same time immersed himself in the study of Eastern philosophy and mysticism so as to bring about a greater understanding and appreciation of both systems.

2. Joseph Campbell, *The Hero with a Thousand Faces.*

3. Bob Dylan, *I Shall Be Free No. 10.*

4. Where relevant, the themes and ideas put forth in certain films will also be presented here, for films are a perfectly valid modern art form. In addition, there has also been a great deal of mutual influence between songwriters and filmmakers.

5. Queen, *Bohemian Rhapsody.*

6. Bob Dylan, *Wallflower.*

PART ONE

Mysticism

CHAPTER 1

THE SPIRIT OF MYSTICISM

That we, as human beings, can experience only a tiny fraction of the phenomena and activity of the universe because of the limitations of our sensory and intellectual faculties is generally accepted as fact. Science has shown that the human ear is only capable of hearing sounds that fall within a tiny band of the vast range of all possible frequencies; the human eye can perceive only an infinitesimal portion of the infinite color spectrum, and so on. In short, we are capable of directly experiencing only those universal forces which fall within the constrained realm of our senses and fixed modes of perception, and this world of sensory phenomena is only the tip of the iceberg, so to speak. In the words of Shakespeare's Hamlet: "There are more things in heaven and earth, Horatio, than are dreamt of in your philosophy."

Mysticism is the effort to transcend these limitations by expanding the mind and opening it up to receive the vast portion of the universe that is hidden from us because of the inadequacy of our sensory apparatus, and because of the filtering processes of the mind. It is the desire to unleash the vast reserves of primal psychic energy latent within every human being, and thus to open up the inner eye of direct perception, and with this awakened eye to behold the blazing light of divine radiance, whose nature is perfect bliss.

According to the sayings of those who have attained such revelation, the true nature of the universe is unity, is oneness. This unity is all-pervading and constitutes the innermost reality of all forms, all life, all thought. True wisdom, then, lies in knowing that we are all part of this transcendent unity, and that our true essence is identical with the essence of the universe, which is uncreated, eternal, and formless, and which radiates through all of creation. All the multifarious forms, appearances, and processes which we perceive with our senses are in reality just different manifestations of this singular omnipresent spirit.

The traditional view of the self as being wholly contained within the body, and of the skin as being the definitive boundary between self and world, must be repudiated entirely. Believing that the body is a detached frame which houses a discrete soul, in much the same way as the hard shell of an oyster encloses a shining pearl, is the great delusion of humanity, and it is the prime contributor to all pain, anxiety and suffering. The Yardbirds said much the same thing in the lyrics below:

> Shapes of things before my eyes
> Just teach me to despise
> Will time make man more wise?
> Here within my lonely frame
> My eyes just hurt my brain
> But will it seem the same?[1]

The world and the body, senses and the objects of sense, are to be seen as simply complementary extensions of one another, with no permanent border between them. Everything is interconnected and intertwined, such that the universe is one indissoluble entity, an integrated and harmonious whole.

Mysticism versus Religion

There is a marked difference between the character of mysticism and that of Western forms of religion, where those religions are founded upon belief in a more or less anthropomorphic God who is essentially a type of benevolent father-figure, and who takes a direct in-

terest and active involvement in the well-being of those who abide by
him and please him with their moral rectitude — the so-called
"interventionist" God. This type of religion is primarily one of worship,
where God is conceived of as a paternal being or power separate from
the worshipper, the Heavenly Father, who must be placated with
prayers, devotion, and righteous moral conduct. The best that can be
hoped for is a positive relationship with this omnipotent God, and the
believer is sustained by the prospect of a blissful afterlife in paradise or
heaven as a reward for good deeds and thoughts in the present life. Sig-
mund Freud has ascribed the origin of this religious outlook to the ide-
alization in early childhood of the father as an all-powerful protector.
He writes:

> Psycho-analysis has made us familiar with the intimate connection
> between the father-complex and belief in God; it has shown us that a
> personal God is, psychologically, nothing other than an exalted fa-
> ther, and it brings us evidence every day of how young people lose
> their religious beliefs as soon as their father's authority breaks down.
> Thus we recognize that the roots of the need for religion are in the
> parental complex; the almighty and just God, and kindly Nature, ap-
> pear to us as grand sublimations of father and mother, or rather as
> revivals and restorations of the young child's ideas of them. Biologi-
> cally speaking, religiousness is to be traced to the small human child's
> long-drawn-out helplessness and need of help; and when at a later
> date he perceives how truly forlorn and weak he is when confronted
> with the great forces of life, he feels his condition as he did in child-
> hood, and attempts to deny his own despondency by a regressive re-
> vival of the forces which protected his infancy.[2]

Mysticism, on the other hand, regards God and all deities as deeply
embedded constituents of the individual's own psyche that have been
projected outward onto the external world, but which are fundamentally contained within the person himself, and are not separate from
him. It does not defer salvation to the afterlife, but aims for it in this
lifetime, here on earth, by union with the omnipresent One, the Supreme Soul. Its highest goal is identity with God, not worship of him,
and its ultimate aim is best described in the words from the Mundaka

Upanishad:[3] "In truth who knows God becomes God."[4] Thus the dichotomy between the two outlooks is that between identity and worship, between communion and placation. The lines below, sung by Bob Marley, illustrate this difference beautifully:

> *Most people think great God will come from the sky*
> *Take away everything, and make everybody feel high*
> *But if you know what life is worth*
> *You will look for yours on earth.[5]*

No ambiguity here as to which worldview Marley subscribed to. He was, after all, in the title of one of his own songs, a "natural mystic."

Thus, the religious point of view places faith in the grace and mercy of God, the wholly other, who dispenses redemption and salvation from on high. The classical Eastern traditions, in contrast, believe that man alone can bring about his highest development, and they emphasize *self*-redemption through experiencing God in every fiber of one's being.

In Christianity, the identification between God and man is said to have occurred only in one specific instance, that of Jesus Christ, and therefore it is outright heresy to subscribe to the mystical view that this divine union is possible, in fact highly desirable, for every single person. Judeo-Christian theology regards God in patriarchal and monarchical terms, and for an individual to claim the position of God for himself is tantamount to a mere mortal arrogating for himself the throne of supreme ruler and controller of the universe. This is, of course, not at all what the mystics mean when they talk about identification and oneness with the Godhead, for they conceive of it in entirely different terms: as a subtle, formless, and all-pervading eternal spirit that is at the same time the inmost self of every person. This oneness is in actuality the natural condition of all things but this fact has been completely obscured and muddled, so that a thorough readjusting of consciousness and cleansing of perception is needed to become fully and deeply aware of it. To the Eastern mind, praying to a heavenly God-King will get you nowhere, for all worship and faith of this kind is directed outwards into the illusory world. Belief in a divine protector may provide solace and sustenance to the faithful in this lifetime, but it certainly does not lead to everlasting salvation.

A story is told in India of an ardent follower of the great god Shiva.[6] This follower was so devoted to his Lord that he placed an idol of him in the center of his home, and every morning he would walk outside, circling the house for an hour with eyes closed and hands raised up to the skies, all the while chanting the name of Shiva. Yet, for all his prayers and devotion, the man was never rewarded by Shiva with any favor or special consideration. Parvati, Shiva's wife, was indignant when she came to know of the callous indifference Shiva showed to his most faithful and dedicated follower, and chastised him for not being more charitable towards the man. To mollify her, and to prove his point, Shiva agreed to shower him with largesse the very next day.

The following morning, when the devotee began his daily routine of walking around his house, Shiva placed a large bag of gold coins at his front doorstep. The man, however, had his eyes closed the whole time and only opened them when he was back indoors, and the bag of coins remained undiscovered outside his house.

The message in this story is clear. Those who remain blinded to the sublime by uncritical adherence to ostensible religious forms and images will never discover the bounty of divine knowledge that lies waiting for them at their doorstep. As Bob Dylan once sang:

> *How many times must a man look up*
> *Before he can see the sky?*[7]

To look up and see the sky, to see the world from a universal perspective rather than from a limited human one, has always been the unwavering aim of the mystics, who refuse to be distracted or misled by the arrays of gods and demons that they have long recognized are merely projections, or productions, of the contents of the human psyche. The mind is seen to have two very different aspects: the personal aspect, which is responsible for our day-to-day experiences and thoughts, and the universal aspect, which encompasses all of creation and which is contained within every form of life. It is only because people are entangled in and caught up with the personal aspect that the universal is lost from sight.

In Greek mythology, Daedalus, the great inventor and artificer, was commissioned by King Minos, of Crete, to build a labyrinth so complex that no one could find his way out. This was to be used to pen up the Minotaur, a grotesque monster, to securely ensconce him in a prison from which he could never escape. Then Theseus took upon himself the task of slaying this monster, but he ran the risk of being trapped in the labyrinth himself. Ariadne, who had fallen in love with him, approached Daedalus for help. Daedalus gave her a ball of thread to give to Theseus. He was to tie one end of it to the entrance of the labyrinth, so that it would then unwind with him as he went further in. Theseus followed these instructions, and after he killed the Minotaur he was able to retrace his steps by following the unraveled thread back to the entrance. Later, as events conspired, Daedalus himself became imprisoned in a tower in his own labyrinth by King Minos, and since all routes by land and sea were heavily guarded, his only means of escape was by air. So, he made himself a pair of wings out of feather and wax, and with these soared across the sea to freedom.

Interpreted mystically, the labyrinth represents the circumscribed personal mind, specific to a given individual, who is forever groping helplessly in the dark and tortuous passages of deluded thought and perception. However, once he grasps the thread of Ariadne, he is led out of his miserable bondage, and once delivered he can soar on his new-found wings above the former prison that was his own creation. The thread represents the symbols and psychic forces that are needed to escape the self-created labyrinth, and the wings of the mystic are his awakened inner vision, by means of which he rises above all illusions and fallacies (which his own mind had generated) into the Universal Mind, the common center of humanity. Once liberated, he has no more use for gods and deities, for they were only needed to lead the way out of the labyrinth, and they have no utility now that he is soaring free, having himself attained the highest, infinite Godhead.

All this is not to say that the mystical tradition is bereft of deities or superhuman beings. On the contrary, Eastern religions such as Hinduism and Buddhism are often replete with a dazzling cornucopia of gods and demons who directly influence the outcome of human endeavors, and who must therefore be propitiated with sacrifices and offerings. However, these deities are not regarded as the ultimate power or highest divinity, but as simply belonging to a level that is one step higher than man in the intricate hierarchical ordering of the universe. At the highest level, in fact at every single level, is the One ever-present Spirit, the subtlest and deepest ground of all things, from the immortal gods to the lowliest creatures.

Any one out of the multitude of gods may, at any time, be elevated in status over the others,[8] but it is always understood that this god is only a temporary and expedient representative of the unmanifest spirit of all life. Rigid belief in him or her is only a substitute for a direct understanding of the higher reality that he/she symbolizes. Western religions usually defer this understanding to the hereafter, whereas the East looks for it in the here and now.

It is illustrative to consider the case of the ancient Greeks and Romans, who also had an impressive array of gods and demons in their pantheon. Even though very few people today believe in the actual existence of Zeus, Hermes, Poseidon, et al.,[9] philosophers and thinkers to this day draw inspiration and insight from these tales of old and look to discover in them ever deeper layers of meaning. Even though literal belief in these figures has by and large ceased, and people no longer sacrifice fatted heifers to the denizens of Mount Olympus, their symbolic significance remains undiminished and they refer to still-extant forces within the human psyche that are constant and unvarying. They speak with the voice of eternity, and therefore live on even after their exterior forms have been abandoned.

The Mystical Life

Given the nature of mysticism and its marked difference from the nature of conventional, organized religion, it follows that simply observing certain customs, rituals, or ceremonials in no way brings one closer to God. What is needed, instead, is a constant state of immersion in the wonder of being, the joy of existence, and an ongoing effort to widen one's consciousness and heighten receptivity to that which is imperceptible and intangible.

An incessant sense of yearning and a gnawing feeling of something lacking in one's knowledge are necessary to prod the weary soul along on the harsh and lonely journey to the regions of pure, distilled being. Without the constant searching and untiring effort born of the spirit of self-inquiry, there is an inevitable slip into inertia and into all-too-familiar patterns of behavior and thought. The lines below, from the U2 song *I Still Haven't Found What I'm Looking For*, communicate perfectly this striving to reach the pinnacle of conscious illumination, and the dissatisfaction felt until that perfect state is achieved:

> *I have climbed the highest mountains*
> *I have run through the fields*
> *Only to be with you*
> *Only to be with you...*
> *I have kissed honey lips*
> *Felt the healing in her fingertips*
> *It burned like fire*
> *This burning desire*
> *I have spoken with the tongue of angels*
> *I have held the hand of a devil*
> *It was warm in the night*
> *I was cold as a stone*
> *But I still haven't found what I'm looking for.*

These words reflect a search that runs the gamut of human emotions, feelings and sensations — from temptation to desire and even to a Faustian pact[10] — but still the sought-after vision remains elusive. Without intense training and proper guidance under the care of a spiritual master (*guru*) the search remains misdirected and unfocussed, and much time and energy is wasted in vain efforts. An exclusive and single-minded concentration and energy on the task at hand is essential, for which the bonds of worldly attachments and relationships must be completely severed. The preferred method in ancient India was to undertake exile (*sanyas*) in the forest, and there to engage in deep contemplation (*dhyana*) until at last one reached the dawn of ultimate realization.

The Buddha was born a crown prince and grew up in the very lap of luxury, but renounced that life of indulgence after being confronted with the harsh realities of sickness, old age, and death. He then experimented with the other extreme — austere asceticism and severe physical discomfort — but soon grew disillusioned with that path as well and proclaimed that true wisdom lay in following the Middle Way, between self-mortification and extravagance, while keeping in mind the doctrine of the Four Noble Truths.[11]

In India, at some point, it was recognized that, while seeking illumination was the highest and noblest pursuit, it was simply not feasible for the average person to renounce the world and his family and to retire into the contemplative solitude required for such an enormously difficult task. Thereafter it was stated that one could reach the exalted state by keeping one's thoughts and mind always on God while going about one's daily tasks and being otherwise engaged in life and society. As long as a person performed his duties selflessly, without hungering after the rewards of his labor but instead offering them up to God, all the while steadfast and unwavering in his devotion, then enlightenment and Nirvana could also be his. Then for him, as for spiritual adepts, the seemingly impenetrable wall in his mind would shatter into smithereens, and find him basking in the incomparable effulgence of the Heavenly light.

We turn once again to a story in Hindu mythology to illustrate the point. According to the story, the divine sage Narada considered himself to be unsurpassed in his devotion to the god Vishnu,[12] and not a moment passed when he did not sing the praises of Vishnu or fervently chant his name. Vishnu, however, told him that an even more devout and pious follower existed: an ordinary mortal. Furthermore, this follower was not even a brahmin (priest) but was a simple farmer who tilled the soil. Narada could scarce believe that a common man, a rustic villager at that, could possibly be more devoted to Vishnu than himself, and asked Vishnu to show him this extraordinary person. Vishnu took Narada down to Earth and pointed out to him the man, who was busy at work in his fields.

Narada observed his rival for a day, then returned to Heaven to speak to Vishnu about what he had seen. He laughed and said that he had paid close attention to the farmer for one whole day, during which time the fellow had barely repeated the name of Vishnu a dozen times, only taking a break once every hour or so from his work in the field to remember his Lord. Why, Narada repeated the name of Vishnu more times in an hour than the simpleton did in a day! How could the two of them even be compared?

Vishnu remained silent through all of this and made no reply. Instead, he said that he had a task that he wanted Narada to perform. He gave him a clay pot filled to the brim with oil and asked him to walk a mile and back while balancing the pot on his head, without spilling a drop. This was an exceedingly challenging task which required strength as well as great skill and coordination, and it absorbed all of Narada's attention. He took each step with the utmost care and circumspection, and heaved a sigh of relief when, after more than two hours, the job was accomplished and not a drop of oil had escaped from the pot.

Vishnu then asked him how many times he had chanted the name of his Lord while he was performing his balancing act. Narada was astonished at the question, and replied that he had not once done so. He had not had a moment's respite from the task at hand to be able to spare a thought for anything else! How could he possibly be expected to divert his mind from such a demanding task? But, Vishnu said, the poor farmer was doing precisely that. He toiled from dawn to dusk, doing backbreaking work, on which the well-being and security of his family depended. Yet, in spite of the importance and demands of his labors, he still made time once an hour to stop and give reverence to Vishnu. What greater devotion could there be? On the other hand, Narada, even when he had been occupied with something relatively inconsequential, was unable to put it aside even once in two hours for that same purpose. After hearing this, the light dawned on Narada and he saw the wisdom of Vishnu's words. He agreed that the person who worked honestly and selflessly at his duties, and took time from the many pressing responsibilities of daily life to remember the Lord and ponder the ageless mysteries, was indeed the greatest of all followers.

A slightly more structured and formal system designed to assist people in regulating and balancing all the aspects of their lives was laid out in the *Laws of Manu*, a book of codes and rules for the ordering of society written in India around 200 B.C. It prescribed that life be divided into four stages. In the first stage, one is a student of religion and studies the sacred texts under the supervision of a teacher. In the second stage, one marries, begets children (preferably sons), and assumes household duties (*grihasti*). The third stage is that of the hermit who withdraws from the world into the forest, and there acquires concentration of mind, loses attachments and becomes purely spiritual. The last stage of life is that of the holy man, or *sanyasi*, when the final liberation and absorption in the Infinite is achieved.

Detachment, Renunciation, *Wu-Wei*

In Eastern philosophy, attachment[13] to the ever-changing and impermanent external forms of objects and material things is the root cause of sorrow, and release of the spirit can only be accomplished by breaking the bonds of desire that chain us to these outward appearances. The ideal state of existence is one of detachment from the objects and relationships around which our lives ordinarily revolve and, in this state of imperviousness to the outer world, of quieting the thought processes and spontaneous productions of the mind. In this way one achieves *samadhi*, the Sanskrit word for the ultimate goal of meditation: union and identification with the universal Absolute, the thought-transcendent monad.

In the whirling rage of passions, desires, and vain hopes that darken one's existence, one must find the eye of the storm and remain steadfast within it. The passions can be compared to a wind that causes ripples on the surface of a lake, thus causing the objects reflected in it to appear broken up and disjointed. To still the passions is to calm the perturbing wind, and then all things be seen accurately reflected in the clear, placid waters. The Bhagavad Gita, the classical text of Hinduism, elucidates further the nature of detachment:

> For when the mind becomes bound to a passion of the wandering senses, this passion carries away man's wisdom, even as the wind drives a vessel on the waves.

The man who therefore in recollection withdraws his senses from the pleasures of sense, his is a serene wisdom.[14]

The mind needs to be always in the same state of quietude amongst the ever-changing circumstances of life, and should retain the same equanimity in the midst of both the joys and sorrows of the world, which are transient and therefore should not be vested with any importance. Most people, however, spend their lives in the vain pursuit of material goods, physical pleasure, career advancement, or any of a number of similarly outward-directed activities in the search for lasting fulfillment. In the song *(I can't get no) Satisfaction*, The Rolling Stones spoke of the futility of attempting to find true contentment through the temporary gratification offered by consumer products and sensual pleasures, i.e. the sense-objects of the external world. In the same vein is Bob Dylan's snarling aphorism, "Money doesn't talk, it swears,"[15] warning against the corrupting power of wealth and the hollowness of a life lived in the singular pursuit of material riches. He states the case more powerfully in the song, *Masters of War*:

> *Let me ask you one question*
> *Is your money that good?*
> *Will it buy you forgiveness?*
> *Do you think that it could?*
> *I think you will find*
> *When your death takes its toll*
> *All the money you made*
> *Will never buy back your soul.*

While these invectives hurled against crass materialism can be construed as cultural and political statements in general, and anti-capitalist in particular, they also lend themselves to interpretations on the metaphysical plane as warnings against chaotic, misdirected activity and false priorities.

A prominent concept in Taoist philosophy is that of *wu-wei*, or non-interfering, non-destructive action. The ideal state of existence is the joyful harmony of the individual with Tao, or the Way of Nature and all things, such that the individual acts in accordance with the Tao and does not take any action that is contrary to it. He simply lets things follow their course, and does not meddle with the smooth operating of nature. The Tao Te Ching explains:

> *Therefore the sage manages affairs without action*
> *And spreads doctrines without words.*
> *All things arise, and he does not turn away from them.*[16]

By following the path of *wu-wei*, one becomes highly attentive and watchful, simply accepting things as they are, not as one wants them to be. The following lines by John Lennon perfectly demonstrate this philosophy in action, and no Taoist sage could argue against these sentiments:

> *People asking questions lost in confusion*
> *Well I tell them there's no problem, only solutions*
> *They shake their heads and look at me as if I've lost my mind*
> *I tell them in I'm no hurry*
> *I'm just sitting here doing time*
> *I'm just sitting here watching the wheels go round and round*
> *I really love to watch them roll*
> *No longer riding on the merry-go-round*
> *I just had to let it go.*[17]

The observer sits, calm and detached, and watches the processes (wheels) of nature in motion without meddling or trying to alter them. There is no hurried activity or meddlesome intrusion with the Tao ("no longer riding on the merry-go-round") and one simply exults in the joy of *being*, without any compulsion to *do*. Any problems that may arise are left to sort themselves out. Only by yielding the conscious will, and letting go the desire to be an active agent and to affect the outcome of events, can the Tao be understood. The moment one tries to assert oneself or dominate the surroundings, the Tao is irretrievably lost.

To other people, the most highly enlightened Taoist sage often appears to be a great fool or simpleton (as Lennon testifies) because of his lack of activity and seeming stupefaction and disinterestedness in the affairs of the world. What they do not realize is that this passiveness or quietude masks an oceanic serenity which comes from knowing the Tao and following it, and letting others follow theirs. This is the highest wisdom, the beacon of light in the darkness. The Beatles sang:

When I find myself in times of trouble
Mother Mary[18] comes to me
Speaking words of wisdom
Let it be
And in my hour of darkness
She is standing right in front of me
Speaking words of wisdom
Let it be.[19]

Everything is endowed with its own nature, its own Tao or *dharma*,[20] which is unique to it, and to act in a manner that is at variance with it can only lead to inner dissonance and turmoil. A human being cannot follow the Tao of a monkey, or a snake, or even of another human being. He can only follow his own course, but first he must find what that course is. This can only happen when he gives up useless strivings and resistances within himself, does not try to force himself to think or act in a certain way, and simply lets his nature flow from within, unimpeded by his interfering will and directing ego; in short, he lets it be. He strives to become like a flowing stream that has no obstacles in its path, or a blade of grass that blows wherever the wind chooses to take it. This is what is implied in the following lines by Queen:

I'm just poor boy, I need no sympathy
Because I'm easy come, easy go
Little high, little low
Any way the wind blows
Doesn't really matter to me.[21]

The ideal conditions for abiding by *wu-wei* are silence, stillness, and non-aggression, such that a person is motivated to act not according to his or her own petty motives, but in accordance with the larger, unitary scheme of things. In this way he becomes a medium through which the forces of the universe flow unimpeded. The Tao Te Ching says:

> *He who takes action fails.*
> *He who grasps things loses them.*
> *For this reason the sage takes no action and therefore does not fail.*
> *He grasps nothing and therefore does not lose anything.*

Bob Dylan's 1967 classic song, *Like a Rolling Stone*, contains the memorable line,

> *When you got nothing, you got nothing to lose.*

which, for good reason, remains perhaps his most well-known and enduring. This is a modern Western philosophical and poetic rendering of the ancient Indian idea of *aparigraha*, or "non-possession," and its proximity to the view stated in the Tao Te Ching before it is nothing short of astonishing. At the heart of the concept of *aparigraha* lies the idea that ownership of objects and goods leads to a weighing down of the soul, and so prevents its release from the chains of the world and the bonds of desire. Therefore, wealth and ownership of property are to be eschewed. This principle manifests itself in the renunciation and world-denial of the ascetic and the monk.

Most recently, Mahatma Gandhi attempted a synthesis of the practice of *aparigraha* with political and social activism, and at the time of his death he had only a handful of possessions, such as his reading glasses, prayer book, walking stick, and slippers. Thus, the renunciation of worldly goods and pleasures is believed to be akin to shedding weight from a hot-air balloon, so that the soul may rise like the unburdened balloon to the heavenly sphere of the Universal Soul, in which all mortal souls are grounded.

It is interesting to note the contrast between this view and that of Western religions, where the goal of renunciation is different; it is usually that of a reward in the afterlife for the deprivations undertaken in this life. Freud has said that renunciation, as enshrined in Western religious doctrine, has as its psychological counterpart the reaction of the reality-principle against the pleasure-principle. In his theory, the *pleasure-principle* moves us to seek nothing but pleasure via the satisfaction of all our instinctual impulses, without any regard to the consequences, and withdraws from any event that causes unpleasure. However, at some point in our development it is tempered by the introduction into the psychological framework of the *reality-principle*, which injects a consideration for practical matters, necessities, and conditions in the external world, and thus tries to save the individual from the destructive indulgence of every potentially dangerous wish and fantasy that seizes him.

The introduction of the reality-principle does not imply a complete renunciation of pleasure, but simply promises pleasure at a later date. It is this substitution of the reality-principle for the pleasure-principle in the individual's mental process, the foregoing of immediate pleasure and the postponement of satisfaction, that corresponds to the religious doctrine of renunciation of earthly pleasures. In Freud's words:

> Just as the pleasure-ego can do nothing but wish, work for a yield of pleasure, so the reality-ego need do nothing but strive for what is useful and guard itself against damage. Actually the substitution of the reality principle for the pleasure principle implies no deposing of the pleasure principle, but only a safeguarding of it. A momentary pleasure, uncertain in its results, is given up, but only in order to gain along the new path an assured pleasure at a later time. But the endopsychic impression made by this substitution has been so powerful that it is reflected in a special religious myth. The doctrine of reward in the after-life for the — voluntary or enforced — renunciation of earthly pleasures is nothing other than a mythical projection of this revolution in the mind. Following consistently along these lines, religions have been able to effect absolute renunciation of pleasure in this life by means of the promise of compensation in a future existence...[22]

Footnotes

1. The Yardbirds, *Shapes of Things.*
2. S. Freud, *Leonardo da Vinci and a Memory of His Childhood.*
3. The Upanishads are a series of Hindu scriptures put down in Sanskrit between 800 and 400 B.C. They are spiritual treatises that were transmitted by enlightened masters to their disciples. The word *Upanishad* translates as "sitting at the feet of a master."
4. All quotations from the Upanishads are taken from the translation by Juan Mascaro, *Penguin Classics* edition.
5. Bob Marley, *Get Up Stand Up.* It is worth noting here the similarity between these lines and a position stated by Freud, albeit with an important difference. While Freud was staunchly opposed to conventional religious beliefs (he famously called religion the "universal obsessional neurosis of humanity"), he was certainly no mystic either. He wanted to replace irrational belief in religious precepts (which he called "illusions") not by a mystical outlook, but by a rational, intellectual, scientific approach which would liberate the minds of men and improve their lot in this world. With that in mind, here are Freud's wishful words from his *Future of an Illusion:*

   > By withdrawing their expectations from the other world and concentrating all their liberated energies into their life on earth, they [men] will probably succeed in achieving a state of things in which life will become tolerable for everyone and civilization no longer oppressive to anyone.

6. Shiva is one of the triad of gods that compromise the Hindu trinity (or *trimurti*) of Brahma, Vishnu, and Shiva. This triad represents the dynamic interplay of forces always at work in the cosmos. Brahma is the creator of the worlds, Vishnu their preserver, and Shiva their destroyer. Shiva's function, however, should not be seen as that of malevolent destruction, but that of an indispensable removal of the debris and dead wood that would otherwise prevent creation and subvert the smooth functioning of the worlds. The cocoon must be destroyed for the butterfly to emerge.
7. Bob Dylan, *Blowin' in the Wind.*
8. This selective elevation of one god above others is known as *henotheism.*
9. According to legend, Emperor Julian of Constantinople was the last to worship the Olympians, and when he died in A.D. 363, Zeus and the gods were told by the Fates to leave Olympus. Zeus then destroyed the place with a thunderbolt and they all went off to live among common folk.
10. This calls to mind the legend of Robert Johnson, who many argue was the

greatest blues musician of all time, and whose story has acquired the status of a modern myth. According the story, Johnson made a pact with the devil, to whom he sold his soul in exchange for his almost supernatural musical talents. Rock superstars such as Keith Richards, Jimi Hendrix, and Eric Clapton cite Johnson as a prime influence in their music.

11. The Four Noble Truths are, briefly: 1) All life is sorrowful; 2) The cause of sorrow (*dukha*) is desire; 3) Cessation of sorrow can come about by the renunciation of desire; 4) The eightfold path, which leads to the cessation of sorrow, consists of right belief, right aspiration, right speech, right conduct, right means of livelihood, right endeavor, right mindfulness, right meditation.

12. The preserver of the worlds (see Footnote 6 in this chapter).

13. *Trishna*, in Sanskrit. This also translates as thirst, desire, craving, clinging, or longing.

14. All quotations from the Bhagavad Gita taken from the translation by Juan Mascaro, *Penguin Classics* edition.

15. Bob Dylan, *It's Alright Ma (I'm only bleeding)*.

16. All quotations from the Tao Te Ching taken from the translation *The Way of Lao Tzu*, by Wing-tsit Chan.

17. John Lennon, *Watching The Wheels*.

18. This is not, as is widely believed, a reference to the Virgin Mary but to Paul McCartney's mother, who died when he was fourteen.

19. The Beatles, *Let It Be*.

20. *Dharma* is a Sanskrit word that is difficult to translate because it has multiple meanings and is used in numerous contexts. Some translations which convey the meaning of this word are "moral order" "righteousness", "guiding principle", "religious law", "duty", and "inner nature".

21. Queen, *Bohemian Rhapsody*.

22. S. Freud, *Formulations on Two Principles of Mental Functioning*.

CHAPTER 2

THE NATURE OF THE WORLD AND THE SELF

The World as Illusion

The music of John Lennon, with The Beatles and as a solo artist, offers up a wealth of material for study in the present context since it is heavy with mystical and philosophical overtones. One outstanding example of this is the song *Strawberry Fields Forever*, which contains the lines:

> *Living is easy with eyes closed*
> *Misunderstanding all you see.*

Perhaps no greater and more succinct exposition of the Hindu concept of *Maya* has found expression in popular culture anywhere. According to this concept, which is also to be found in Buddhism, the images of life and the world that unfold before our eyes are illusory and unreal, products of our distorting senses and confounding mental activity. *Maya* is said to be the agent within our mind that causes this illusion, and it must be overcome before any soul awakening can take place.

The true goal of the yogi, or seeker of truth, then, is to transcend the lower plane of ordinary consciousness, with its deluded mode of experiencing the world, and to achieve union with pure consciousness — the Nirvana of Buddhism, and the *moksha* (salvation by escape from the endless cycle of rebirths) of Hinduism. If fact, the word yoga is derived from the Sanskrit word *yuj*, meaning "to yoke," the goal being to yoke the lower, ordinary, consciousness to the higher.

Thus, in our everyday lives we are all living in Strawberry Fields, where,

> *Nothing is real*
> *And nothing to get hung about.*

The similarity between the above lines and the following verses from the Bhagavad Gita, the classical text of Hinduism, is remarkable. The speaker of these words is Krishna, who symbolizes the one Supreme Soul that informs and supports the whole of the universe:

> The unwise think that I am that form of my lower nature which is seen by mortal eyes: they know not my higher nature, imperishable and supreme.
> For my glory is not seen by all: I am hidden by my veil of mystery; and in its delusion the world knows me not, who was never born and for ever I am.

The Tao Te Ching says of this subtle, imperceptible presence:

> *We look at it and we do not see it;*
> *Its name is The Invisible.*
> *We listen to it and do not hear it;*
> *Its name is The Inaudible.*
> *We touch in and do not find it;*
> *Its name is The Subtle (formless).*

In Christianity, also, the workings of *Maya* are alluded to in the maxim:

> The Kingdom of the Father is spread upon the earth and men do not see it.[1]

Men do not see it because their minds are clouded and in a constant state of agitation, darting forever from this object to that, from past memories to future dreams, never constant and still, never focused on the present moment. They look for something permanent and eternal since all around them is impermanent and transient, but they mistakenly look for it within the familiar, limited environment of their prosaic existence which is bounded by time and space, instead of turning their gaze inwards to the center of their own selves, which is immortal and timeless, but which remains hidden from them and proves utterly elusive when pursued by intellectual or analytical methods. In the introduction to his translation of the Upanishads, Juan Mascaro writes.

The silent voice of the Eternal is perpetually whispering in us his melodies everlasting. The radiance of the Infinite is everywhere, but our ears cannot hear and our eyes cannot see: the Eternal cannot be grasped by the transient senses or the transient mind.

In the song *Dear Prudence*, The Beatles also drew upon a similar conception of people being oblivious to the glory that surrounds them, blind to the ecstatic vision of universal oneness that shows itself to those who are able to open the mystic inner eye of revelation:

Dear Prudence
Open up your eyes
Dear Prudence
See the sunny skies.

To open one's (subtle) eyes and ears requires the faculty of *viveka* (refined discrimination, discernment), such that it becomes possible to differentiate between truth and illusion, gold and base metal. Once one is in possession of *viveka*, it becomes patently clear that it is *Maya* which creates the profusion of shapes and images that swirl before our eyes and which impress themselves upon our senses. If, however, these images are not seen for the empty and insubstantial forms that they are, the mind becomes transfixed by them and is consigned to remain in perpetual ignorance.

In the song *Carnival*, Natalie Merchant gives voice to the nagging doubt which at one point or another makes itself felt to most people, whether we are really, truly cognizant of the nature of what we per-

ceive, or are instead under the spell of some great cosmic hoax originat-
ing in our mind:

Have I been blind
Have I been lost
Inside my self and my own mind?
Hypnotized, mesmerized
By what my eyes have seen·

Have I been wrong
Have I been wise
To shut my eyes and play along?
Hypnotized, paralyzed
By what my eyes have found
By what my eyes have seen.

Form and Matter

In the Samkhya philosophy of Hinduism, the Universal Mind is
said to have two different aspects — *saguna*, with form and properties,
and *nirguna*, formless and without properties.[2] In its *saguna* aspect, it is
seen as *prakriti* (corporeal matter) which is manifest as form (*rupa*) and
shape, and which possesses attributes, or *gunas*. These *gunas* are: *sattva*
(purity, goodness), *rajas* (action, energy), and *tamas* (darkness, inertia).
The characteristics of everything in the world are determined by the
manner in which these three elemental *gunas* combine. In its *nirguna* aspect, on the contrary, the creative and animating all-consciousness is
devoid of form and attributes. It is completely indescribable, and references to it must of necessity be highly abstract and negative. In attempting to talk about it one can only say, *neti, neti* — "neither this, nor
that."

The *saguna* world is the one we normally see and identify with, but
it is in fact just a product of the mind and is completely dependent on
each individual. Supporting and suffusing the *saguna* is the *nirguna*, the

hypostasis which is the source of all manifested forms and sentient matter. To reach the *nirguna*, the *saguna* must be pierced to the core, and for this the individual mind has to be sacrificed, for it creates the *saguna* universe through the action of *Maya*.

The philosopher-mathematician Descartes conducted an investigation into the nature of matter and its properties, and came to similar conclusions (although he drew different inferences from them, since he was trying to logically prove the existence of a benevolent God). He attempted to free himself as completely as he could from subliminal prejudices and preconceived notions, and to apprehend objects and sensations with a mind that had become, in effect, a *tabula rasa*. With this new unjaundiced eye he set about to examine what exactly was the nature of the objects he saw and experienced all around him, and chose a lump of wax as a representative subject of his investigation. Of the wax he wrote:

> It has been taken quite recently from the honeycomb; it has not yet lost all the honey flavor. It retains some of the scent of the flowers from which it was collected. Its color, shape, and size are manifest. It is hard and cold; it is easy to touch. If you rap on it with your knuckle it will emit a sound. In short, everything is present in it that appears needed to enable a body to be known as distinctly as possible. But notice that, as I am speaking, I am bringing it closer to the fire. The remaining traces of the honey flavor are disappearing; the scent is vanishing; the color is changing; the original shape is disappearing. Its size is increasing; it is becoming liquid and hot; you can hardly touch it. And now, when you rap on it, it no longer emits any sound. Does the same wax still remain? I must confess that it does; no one denies it; no one thinks otherwise. So what was there in the wax that was so distinctly grasped? Certainly none of the aspects that I reached by means of the senses. For whatever came under the senses of taste, smell, sight, touch or hearing has now changed; and yet the wax remains.[3]

The essence of the wax, and of all matter, lies not in its properties, which are constantly changing and transforming, but in the invisible spirit that infuses it. Matter, then, merely represents different levels of concentration or condensation of this pervasive field where and when it chooses to display itself.

The ideas of *saguna*, *nirguna*, and those of Descartes find a parallel in the quantum field theory of modern theoretical physics. In this theory, the underlying entity of all material objects is the quantum field, a con-tinuum present everywhere in space, and the presence of matter is merely a disturbance or imperfection of the field at a particular place. The field is the only reality, everything else being just variations in its intensity. Thus, *nirguna* equals quantum field, and *saguna* equals distur-bance or condensation of the quantum field.

Albert Einstein, in his theory of relativity, proposed that mass is just a form of energy. The amount of energy bound up in the mass of an object is given by the equation: $E = mc^2$, where m is the mass of the ob-ject, and c is the speed of light. Since mass, or matter, is just a form of energy, and since one form of energy transforms easily into another, it follows that matter does not now need to be seen as static and fixed, but rather as dynamic and freely moving within the parent energy field. Fritjof Capra, the particle physicist and modern interpreter of Eastern mystical thought, writes:

> The discovery that mass is nothing but a form of energy has forced us to modify our concept of a particle in an essential way. In modern physics, mass is no longer associated with a material substance, and hence particles are not seen as consisting of any basic "stuff," but as bundles of energy. Since energy, however, is associated with activity, with processes, the implication is that the nature of subatomic parti-cles is intrinsically dynamic.[4]

All the ideas discussed so far present a picture of pure spirit de-scending to the world of matter and substance via temporary, localized concentrations of its energy. This new way of thinking can also help to shed light on the Hindu concept of an *avatar*, the incarnation of a divine being or deity in human or animal form. It really represents the descent of sheer energy or spirit into perishable matter. Sri Aurobindo, the re-nowned contemporary Indian thinker, put it elegantly when he said:

All life here is a stage in an unfolding progressive evolution of a spirit that has involved itself in matter and is laboring to manifest itself in that reluctant substance. This is the whole secret of earthly existence.[5]

What is striking is the fact that these esoteric and abstruse theories have been articulated in one of the most successful popular music albums of all time, Pink Floyd's legendary *Dark Side of the Moon*.[6] Consider the following extracts from a song on the album:

And all that you touch
All that you see
All that you taste
All you feel...

All that is now
All that is gone
All that's to come
And everything under the sun is in tune
But the sun is eclipsed by the moon.[7]

This introduces the concepts of solar consciousness and lunar consciousness. Like the sun, solar consciousness is fiery and radiant, and illuminates the entire world. It is a blazing forth of pure energy, and is to be identified with the highest self, with what the Buddhists call *dharmakaya*, the divine body of truth, shining and radiant. Lunar consciousness, in contradistinction, is engaged in the limited field of space and time, of birth and death, and is the consciousness incarnate in all beings in the world of *prakriti*. However, just as the light of the moon is but reflected solar light, so lunar consciousness is but a reflection and shadow of solar consciousness. The world of ordinary experience is to then be regarded as the result of a sort of solar eclipse in which the eternal (*nirguna*) has been blotted out by the temporal (*saguna*).

The Unity of all Consciousness

Given that the true nature of the world and our selves is concealed from us by the filtering and distorting layer of the senses, what, then, is reality? Reality, as professed by enlightened souls from time immemorial, lies in the fact that beyond the world of the senses and ordinary consciousness, everything is One. There is no duality, no "I" and "you," and nothing is separate from anything else. There is no differentiation between subject and object except that which is produced by the mind, which is incapable of experiencing the whole and must therefore break it up into assimilable parts.

The underlying unity of all consciousness, in fact of the entire universe at large, is a tenet of Eastern thought, from Hinduism and Buddhism to Taoism, and also forms a large portion of primitive and tribal thought throughout the world and through all ages. The universality of this insight and its applicability to the modern age of science and technology has also been reinforced by certain principles of mathematics and recent corroborating discoveries in sub-atomic physics, as we will presently see.

According to this idea, the action of Maya deludes us and prevents us from seeing the universe as it actually is — an infinite, formless, timeless, indestructible unity, under which the seemingly endless variety of all external forms is completely subsumed, and into which they ultimately dissolve. The soul, or essence, of every individual being is identical with the one Universal Soul that permeates everything, and our ordinary experience of being separate from it, and all that surrounds us, is the result of falling prey to Maya and failing to understand who we really are. It is avidya (Sanskrit for "ignorance").

An appropriate analogy represents the Universal Spirit as an infinite ocean, and the individual soul as a wave or droplet which momentarily rises up from the vast expanse of water and believes itself to be separate from all the other similarly short-lived droplets. The reality is that there is only one ocean, one soul, one consciousness. The infinity of forms which appears before our mortal eyes is ultimately contained within this higher reality in which all forms are grounded, from which they emanate, and into which they inevitably return. The Katha Upanishad says:

As fire, though one, takes new forms in all things that burn, the Spirit, though one, takes new forms in all things that live. He is within all, and is also outside.

In this scheme of things, even space and time are not considered to be distinct entities, and are seen as merely illusory creations of an ego in the thrall of *Maya*. All pairs of opposites, which are ordinarily considered to be mutually exclusive, are seen as simply being different manifestations of the one and the same causative principle. They are the obverse of each other, two sides of the same coin, and it is only *Maya* that makes us think of them as being irreconcilably different. In modern physics also, relativity theory has unified the previously separate concepts of space and time into a single dimension, giving scientific corroboration to these mystical insights. It is the *Maya*-bewitched mind that, in its ignorance, perceives infinity as limited space and eternity as linear time, and which reduces omniscience to commonplace knowledge. Sri Aurobindo expressed this truth with great clarity when he wrote:

An unknowable which appears to us in many states and attributes of being, in many forms of consciousness, in many activities of energy, this is what Mind can ultimately say about the existence which we ourselves are and which we see in all that is presented to our thought and senses. It is in and through those states, those forms, those activities that we have to approach and know the Unknowable. But if in our haste to arrive at a unity that our mind can seize and hold, if in our insistence to confine the Infinite in our embrace we identify the reality with any one definable state of being however pure and eternal, with any particular attribute however general and comprehensive, with any fixed formulation of consciousness however vast in its scope, with any energy or activity however boundless its application, and if we exclude all the rest, then our thoughts sin against Its unknowableness and arrive not at a true unity but at a division of the Indivisible.[8]

The unity of all things is the central theme of the Upanishads, in which the obliteration of all dualities, is explained via the notion of

Brahman/Atman. Brahman is the fundamental essence, or infinite Spirit, of the universe. Atman is the essence of the individual soul, or the Self. The Upanishads proclaim Brahman and Atman to be one and the same; that is, the spirit of the universe is identical to the spirit of every individual. Thus, God is to be sought not as a distant entity far removed from us, but in the most intimate depths of our own selves. In the story of Svetaketu in the Chandogya Upanishad, Svetaketu's father, who is also his spiritual guide and *guru*, asks him to repeatedly break a seed from the fruit of a tree into pieces until it can be broken no further and nothing can be seen inside it. Then his father initiates Svetaketu into the esoteric mystery of the universe:

> My son, from the very essence in the seed which you cannot see comes in truth this vast banyan tree. Believe me, my son, an invisible and subtle essence is the Spirit of the whole universe. That is Reality. That is Atman. THOU ART THAT.

In Chinese, the word *hsuan-t'ung*, an important principle in Taoist thought, denotes identification of the individual with the universal, and the removal of all distinctions and differentiations. As Chuang Tzu says: "The universe and I exist together, and all things and I are one." This insight of the grand cosmic unity finds expression in Christianity in the dictum "I and the Father are one," where the Father is to be interpreted as a transpersonal monism and not as a personalistic, patriarchal deity.

These metaphysical revelations have also been enunciated in popular music and culture. The opening line of The Beatles' *I Am The Walrus*, below, explicitly asserts the unity and interconnectedness of all life:

> *I am he as you are he as you are me and we are all together.*

In *Instant Karma*, John Lennon sings about transcending everyday existence, with all its attendant pain and suffering, by realizing that our true self is illimitable, is present everywhere, and is not to be confused with the physical body, which is confined to a fixed location in space and a certain age in time. This true self is luminous and glows with an intensity that is beyond the scope of ordinary conception, and it can only be compared with the brightest objects known to mankind: the celestial bodies. Lennon says:

Why in the world are we here?
Surely not to live in pain and fear
Why on earth are you there?
When you're everywhere
Come and get your share

Well we all shine on
Like the moon and the stars and the sun

The lyrics by U2, below, also have strong connotations of a potential state of consciousness in which all contrapositions and demarcations are eliminated, so that all things merge together into a perfectly blended amalgam:

I believe in the Kingdom come
Then all the colors will bleed into one.[9]

This Kingdom, as we have read, is already spread on the earth but we do not see it. We do not see it because we look for it in the world outside instead of within ourselves, within our mind. "Mind," however, has too often been confused with "brain," which is limited and confined to a fixed location within the hollow casing of the cranial cavity. There are innumerable brains at large in the world, but only one Mind, the totality of the self, which stretches out to infinity. The world is merely an extension of this One Mind, only a portion of which is apprehended by any given brain or organ of sense.

The idea of the Universal Mind, of one timeless and eternal soul common to all of humanity, is also expounded by John Steinbeck, in *The Grapes of Wrath*, through the revelation of the preacher Casey, who is a prophetic and shamanistic figure. Casey describes his vision to his friend Tom Joad:

I figgered about the Holy Sperit and the Jesus Road. I figgered, "Why do we got to hang it on God or Jesus? Maybe," I figgered, "maybe it's all men an' all women we love; maybe that's the Holy Sperit — the human sperit — the whole shebang. Maybe all men got one big soul ever'body's a part of. Now I sat there thinkin' it, an' all of a suddent — I knew it. I knew it so deep down that it was true, and I still know it.

Time and Change

All things in the universe are in a constant state of flow and change, and the processes of creation and destruction are engaged in an ongoing dynamic interplay with each other. The cosmos is organic, growing, and fluid, and all static forms seen within it are *Maya*, existing only as evanescent, illusory concepts. All suffering in the world arises from our trying to cling to fixed forms instead of accepting the world as it moves and changes. Our experience of time as linear and constant is also based on error, since time, like space, is only our *Maya*-generated experience and has no validity outside the mind. In fact, linear time belongs to the *saguna*, or vitiated, worldview and acts to shut out Eternity. Plato suggested that eternity is the ideal, and time is but a moving image of it. In speaking of the created world, he said:

> When the father creator saw the creature which he had made moving and living, the created image of the eternal gods, he rejoiced, and in his joy determined to make the copy still more like the original; and as this was eternal, he sought to make the universe eternal, so far as might be. Now the nature of the ideal being was everlasting, but to bestow this attribute in its fullness upon a creature was impossible. Wherefore he resolved to have a moving image of eternity, and when he set in order the heavens, he made this image eternal but moving according to number, while eternity itself rests in unity; and this image we call time.[10]

Becoming too closely identified with the world of clock-measured time, with its dancing images and its merciless forward movement, can only lead to anguish, for linear time has a highly detrimental effect on *prakriti*, matter, to which the ravages of old age, decay, and dilapidation only too clearly attest. By agonizing endlessly about the passage of time and about the impossibility of turning the clock back in order to achieve more than has been done so far, one is caught in a vicious regressive spiral and is drawn ever downward into the quicksand of impossible expectations from which it becomes increasingly difficult to climb out of. The following Pink Floyd lyrics deal with the despondency that results from identifying too closely with chronological time, and from trying desperately to live up to a timetable of accomplishments before the fateful sands of the hourglass run out:

You are young and life is long, and there is time to kill today
And then one day you find, ten years have got behind you
No one told you when to run
You missed the starting gun

And you run and you run to catch up with the sun, but it's sinking
And racing around to come up behind you again
The sun is the same in a relative way, but you're older
Shorter of breath, and one day closer to death

Every year is getting shorter, never seem to find the time
Plans that either come to naught or half a page of scribbled lines
Hanging on in quiet desperation is the English way
The time is gone, the song is over
Thought I'd something more to say...[1]

Again, the sun here represents that which is eternal and unchanging, because the same sun has always shone upon the earth since it was created, and the same sun has warmed and nourished all forms of life since they first appeared. When faced with the immensity of the natural laws of change and impermanence it is easy to throw up one's hands in despair and be simply swept away in the onrush of the inexorable stream of time, but, like all other mind-constructed concepts, earthly time too can be superseded by its original and elemental form if one reaches the clear, undistorted vision of *samadhi*, in which time is seen as but a mere wavelet in the abounding ocean of timelessness. Of ordinary time, David Bowie sang:

I watch the ripples change their size
But never leave the stream
Of warm impermanence.[12]

When the flow of time is parceled out into units of measure, be they seconds, days, or millennia, the unbroken continuum of eternity becomes fragmented and little eddies or whirlpools form within it. All changes and events that occur are merely momentary ripples emanating from these temporary disturbances, and merely represent transitions of energy from one form to another. The ultimate ground of all changes is only arrived at by leaving the stream of warm impermanence and embracing that which is permanent, immutable, and indestructible, of which Plato remarked:

> We say that he "was," he "is," he "will be," but the truth is that "is" alone is properly attributed to him, and that "was" and "will be" only to be spoken of becoming in time, for they are motions, but that which is immovably the same cannot become older or younger by time, nor ever did or has become, or hereafter will be, older or younger, nor is subject at all to any of those states which affect moving and sensible things and of which generation is the cause. These are the forms of time, which imitates eternity and revolves according to a law of number.[13]

So, trapped in this world of ordinary time, of imitated eternity, one is but a puppet in the hands of a mysterious, supernatural force which continually pushes one forward and creates its moving images, providing not the least clue as to who is pulling the strings. So, the recurring refrain in the above David Bowie song is:

Time may change me
But I can't trace time.

The source of all activity and dynamism is always the one energy center which propels and impels everything, and until that is comprehended one will never be able to trace the real origin of the motivating force behind all change and motion. In order to reach this fathomless ocean, in which all activity originates, one needs to rise above the time-bound world of the lower, earthly realm of thought. This helps to explain the following lyrics by the Steve Miller Band:

Time keeps on slipping, slipping, slipping
Into the future

I want to fly like an eagle
To the sea
Fly like an eagle
Let my spirit carry me
I want to fly like an eagle
Till I'm free. [14]

Just as the mighty eagle (which has always represented solar consciousness[15]) soars in the calm and peaceful skies high above the terrestrial world, so the mystic savant uses his spirit power to ascend beyond temporal and mundane consciousness to the rarefied upper regions of the soul, where quantifiable time dissolves like a lump of salt into the eternal sea of Brahman.

The essential thing is to realize that all life and all matter is in a constant cycle of motion and mutual interaction, and that those things that appear to be fixed or static are only phenomenal appearances. Attachment to these appearances can only lead to suffering and sorrow, for they are but apparitions, momentary condensations of the infinite energy field; and since energy is constantly changing and metamorphosing, it is only a matter of time before what is believed to be a firm, durable reality today disintegrates or decays and is recast as something else in the future. This is the cosmic cycle of birth, life, and death which repeats endlessly in life and in the universe, and which is represented by the Hindu trinity of Brahma, Vishnu and Shiva.[16]

The underlying protean, ever-changing quality of that which seems rigid and persistent was expressed by Bob Dylan in *The Times They Are A-Changin'*. This song is almost universally understood as a rallying cry for pressing social and political reform, but the following lines from it could just as easily be referring to the change and flux inherent in a world referenced by discrete quantities of time:

The line it is drawn, the curse it is cast
The slow one now, will later be fast
As the present now, will later be past
The order is rapidly fading
And the first one now, will later be last
For the times they are a-changin'.

The line that is drawn is the delineation of time from eternity, which can only be seen as a curse because of the suffering and disillusionment it entails. Past and present, slow and fast, only come about from the defilement of the timeless, and for those who set undue store by them, the changing of the times will only leave them floundering behind, stranded and alone.

Footnotes

1. *The Gospel According to Thomas.*
2. Samkhya philosophy, because it hypothesizes two radically different aspects of nature, is considered to be one of the very few dualistic schools of thought in Hinduism. However, this philosophy can also been regarded non-dualistically if one identifies the *saguna* world with that of ordinary consciousness, and the *nirguna* world with that of purified consciousness.
3. Descartes, *Meditations on First Philosophy.*
4. Fritjof Capra, *The Tao of Physics.*
5. Sri Aurobindo, *The Life Divine.*
6. It is worth noting that the cover of the album shows a prism breaking up a beam of pure light and splitting it into a rainbow of colors (see Illustration 1). In the same way as a prism, the human mind splits up pure consciousness into the myriad objects that stream forth from it. Just as all the different colors inhere in the pure light, so the various objects we see, and from which we normally dissociate ourselves completely, inhere in the total field of our supra-consciousness.
7. Pink Floyd, *Eclipse.*
8. Sri Aurobindo, *The Life Divine.*
9. U2, *I Still Haven't Found What I'm Looking For.*
10. Plato, *Timaeus.*
11. Pink Floyd, *Time.*
12. David Bowie, *Changes.*
13. Plato, *Timaeus.*
14. Steve Miller Band, *Fly Like An Eagle.*
15. In Greek mythology, the vehicle and symbol of Zeus is the eagle, whose form Zeus himself sometimes assumes when descending to earth. When Hercules was about to be consumed in the funeral pyre, Zeus sent down his eagle so that Hercules could ascend on it to Mount Olympus, where he achieved immortality. Similarly, in Hindu mythology the vehicle of Vishnu is the fabled Garuda, half eagle-half man, whose courageous and indomitable spirit are legendary throughout all the worlds. In Indonesia, where the official state religion is Islam, the national airline is named after this Hindu mythical creature.
16. See Chapter 1, Footnote 6.

CHAPTER 3

AWAKENING OF THE TRUE SELF

Realization of the Great Unity

When a person is in good health, he feels himself to be an organic and completely balanced whole. His body coordinates and regulates its activities spontaneously, and is not experienced as being divided up into its constituent components. Only when the person is sick or is suffering from pain in some part of the body does he feel that part to be somehow separate from the rest, and his attention focuses on it to the exclusion of the rest of the body, until he is relieved of the pain or discomfort. Similarly, the person who has a properly integrated worldview and who sees himself as inseparable from the rest of creation is possessed of psychic well-being, whereas the person whose focus is concentrated on himself and his individual ego is spiritually sick, and remains bound in the chains of ignorance.

But how does one who is not a yogi or a spiritual adept experience the basic unity of all things and transcend the world of ordinary consciousness, of *Maya*, into which all are born? According to ancient India, this can be done by understanding the secret workings of the mind free from the intrusions of the ego, by subduing the thought process, and meditating on the eternal One. Yoga also prescribes specialized breathing exercises (*pranayama*) and specifically designed postures (*asanas*) to that end. The *asanas* train the various parts of the body and unite them with the whole of the mind and spirit. *Pranayama* exercises elevate the spirit such that each inhalation and exhalation becomes the ebb and flow of the universe. After these arduous techniques have been mastered, the ecstatic vision is attained, of which the Bhagavad Gita says:

> Thus joy supreme comes to the Yogi whose heart is still, whose passions are peace, who is pure from sin, who is one with Brahman, with God.

> The Yogi who pure from sin ever prays in this harmony of soul soon feels the joy of Eternity, the infinite joy of union with God.

> He sees himself in the heart of all beings and he sees all beings in his heart. This is the vision of the Yogi of harmony, a vision which is ever one.

The unchecked instincts and impulses of the body and of the lower psychic strata act as tentacles which wrap themselves around the mind, preventing its upward, uplifting movement. The physical, physiological, and spiritual exercises of yoga are a means of breaking free of these choking weeds so that they no longer interfere with the process of higher development. It should, however, be noted that the body is not to be disowned or regarded as abased in any way. Although the bodily passions in their raw and uncontrolled form, when allowed to run wild, are certainly impediments to real, penetrating insight, it is also the case that the instincts are vested with enormous amounts of primal energy which can be, indeed must be, put to work for the refinement of the spirit. When gushing waters flow through the wrong channels they wreak havoc, but when properly directed through the correct channels they provide access to a prodigious force that can be employed for the highest and noblest ends.

Yoga is precisely such an attempt to harness the instinctual energies of the body and to put them to work in the great task of unlocking the full human potential for unity, creativity, and harmony. Hence the great emphasis that yoga places on uniting mind and body such that they work together in synergy toward the goal of realizing Brahman.

Much has been made of the imperviousness of expert yogis to their bodies and what is happening to them, but this in itself is certainly not the end goal of yoga. Indifference to body and world is only a side-effect of the highest mental state, for, as Jung says:

> The fact that the general bodily sensations disappear during the experience suggests that their specific energy has been withdrawn and has apparently gone towards heightening the clarity of consciousness.[1]

All the resources available to the mind must be mustered, because ordinary levels of psychic energy are simply not sufficient for reaching the highest illumination. Just as the diamond is inherent in unrefined carbon but requires great heat and pressure before it acquires its precious and lustrous form, so too the great heat (*tapas*) generated by the assiduous practice of yoga is necessary to liberate the spirit from its internment in the flesh.

By controlling the passions and desires that rage within the breast, and taming the capricious workings of the mind, one can open oneself up to divinity and higher truth. By cultivating serenity, tranquility, and stillness one harmonizes the inner self with the higher forces operating beyond the human sensorium, and can unfold hitherto concealed vistas in the mind that reveal the hidden secret which mankind has hungered for throughout the ages. Taken in this context, the concluding lines to Led Zeppelin's *Stairway To Heaven*, below, are colored with a definite mystical hue:

> *And if you listen very hard*
> *The tune will come to you at last*
> *When all are one and one is all*
> *To be a rock and not to roll.*

Music consists of variations in sound, and sound is formed by vibrations. In Hinduism and Buddhism, the purest and most perfect sound is said to be the mystic syllable "OM," from which all other sounds are formed and which contains within it all the processes and forms of life as well as the different modes of consciousness. It is said to be identical with the Brahman/Atman non-dualistic entity, and it resonates with the vibration that caused the universe to be created out of formlessness at the beginning of time, and that now sustains all these creations.[2] To harmonize the vibration of the self with this supreme cosmic vibration, the mind must be intensely concentrated on it and oblivious to the vagaries of the world, to the vicissitudes of happiness, sorrow, pain and pleasure. It must be silent and steadfast like a rock amidst the raging storm of the sense-bound passions and desires, and to reach this profound state of constant unperturbedness requires unprecedented toil, sacrifice, and discipline.

Ultimately, the goal is to see the sublime truth in the pure light of transcendent knowledge, free from the corrupting influences of the lower consciousness that blinds and blinkers us all. In the secret heart of the soul, when the mind is silenced, centered, and concentrated on the timeless, immortal quintessence of the self, the darkness of delusion is dispelled by the blazing light of true understanding. Like a tiny iceberg under the warm glow of the sun, one melts back into the ocean of pure consciousness. Without the light and the warmth, ignorance and pettiness dominate, and the Ariadne thread which leads us out of the labyrinth of our suffering and misery is forever lost.

The Higher Dimension

Inherent in all these ideas is the assumption that the ordinary mode of consciousness, with all its divisions and distinctions, is insufficient, is even a positive hindrance, to experiencing the transcendent truth. A higher plane of consciousness must be attained before the vision of the Divine can be apprehended in its unmitigated glory. This resplendent vision can only be experienced when the selective filter of consciousness has been removed, before the mind has been, to quote Hamlet, "sicklied o'er with the pale cast of thought."[3] It cannot be appreciated by those for whom the filter is still firmly in place, and whose minds are irresolute in any way.

It is to reach the higher conscious plane, above the time-bound world of fluctuating ego-emanations, where mind, body, and ego are cast aside, that the yogi performs his austerities to subdue the flesh,

50

and the Taoist sage attempts to become supple and pliant like the grass that bends without offering resistance to the billowing breeze, so that he may achieve harmony with the Tao. Fritjof Capra has drawn a parallel between the higher consciousness of the sage and the fourth dimension of space-time in relativity theory, which transcends the ordinary three-dimensional world and in which opposites are united, as is the case in the mystic revelation. He writes:

> Relativity theory is crucial for the description of this world, and in the "relativistic" framework the classical concepts are transcended by going to a higher dimension, the four-dimensional space-time. Space and time themselves are two concepts which had seemed entirely different, but have been unified in relativistic physics. This fundamental unity is the basis of the unification of opposites mentioned above. Like the unity of opposites experienced by the mystics, it takes place on a "higher plane," i.e. in a higher dimension.[4]

It is interesting to consider from this perspective the mathematical concept of a *hyperbody*.[5] A hyperbody is an object with more dimensions than can be directly detected by a being in a lesser-dimensional reality. This being can only visualize a projection, or shadow, of a hyperbody existing in the next higher dimension,[6] but this shadow will of necessity have some element from the original hyperbody that is missing. As an example, let us consider the case of a person who lives in a purely two-dimensional world, a flat plane with no thickness. This person can be told about the third dimension, but has absolutely no way of experiencing it because of his confinement in his limited plane, which prevents him from perceiving depth. He can, however, see the *shadow* of a three-dimensional object, such as a cube, as it falls on his plane, where it will appear as a square or some other two-dimensional figure (depending on the angle of the light source); but this shadow is invariably a vague and insufficient approximation, and some aspect of the original, related to its depth, is destined to remain obscure to him. For the two-dimensional person, a three-dimensional cube is a hyperbody, and will always remain mysterious and unknowable to him in the fullness of its reality.

In the same way human beings, who exist in a three-dimensional world, can have no direct knowledge of a four-dimensional object, but can see a shadow of this object projected onto three dimensions. Illustration 2 shows just such a three-dimensional projection of a four-dimensional cube (also known as a hypercube), which for us is a hyperbody. Transcendent mystical experiences enable one to overcome ordinary human limitations, and to ascend to the higher dimensions where one can directly see these super-dimensional entities. Therefore, the mystical concepts that have been discussed thus far, such as the Universal Mind and the *nirguna* realm, can be understood as four-dimensional hyperbodies which exist on a transcendent plane (hyperspace), and of which we see only shadows or reflections. In their descent to our dimensions they break up and assume solid forms with shapes and attributes, but in their unmodulated essence they are continuous and unbroken. For example, when two or more light sources shine on the same three-dimensional object, such as a flagpole, they cause multiple two-dimensional shadows of differing proportions to appear on the ground, but the cause of all these shadows is the one and the same pole.

Salvador Dali's painting *Crucifixion (Hypercubic Body)*[7] shows Christ nailed to a cross that is in fact a three-dimensional representation of a hypercube.[8] This hypercube representation looks different from the one shown in Illustration 2, but is in fact the same. It is simply a rearrangement of the surfaces. The representation in Dali's painting is made up of eight cubes, four stacked vertically and four more meeting face-to-face with the second highest vertical cube. Just as a two-dimensional cross can be made by unfolding a three-dimensional paper cube, in the same way the three-dimensional cross in the painting is the result of unfolding a hypercube. Furthermore, the pattern on the floor is tessellated like a chessboard, and is in fact the two-dimensional shadow that would be cast if a light source were shone directly over the three-dimensional cross. The pattern is, therefore, the two-dimensional shadow of the cross, which is itself a three-dimensional shadow of a hypercube.

We can now attempt an interpretation of this painting. The hypercube cannot be rendered in its entirety and so it represents the transcendent and incommunicable, for it can never be known completely to ordinary consciousness. The three-dimensional cross is thus its earthly manifestation, and it exists in the spatial reality in which we live as human beings. Since Christ is nailed to this cross, he too is the incarnation of the hyperbody in a lower dimension, the spirit made flesh. He is the three-dimensional representative of the four-dimensional God. His divine origin can be inferred from the fact that he floats suspended above the two-dimensional floor, the material world of delusion and desire in which the image of the hyperbody is diminished and distorted even further from its original form by the reduction of yet another dimension. The woman who is looking up at him symbolizes the seeker of truth, and she stands on a pedestal between the floor and the cross. She has lifted herself partially above the mundane world by her desire for enlightenment, but cannot claim the divinity of Christ.

Christ's suffering on the cross implies that existence in this lower and more limited plane is sorrowful.[9] This sorrow can only be cured by rising above the confines of restricted reality, by the death of the three-dimensional body and the consequent resurrection and ascension to the higher dimension by the assumption of a new spirit-body. This is exactly what happened in the case of Christ.

The Christian Church would claim that this ascension to the astral plane of consciousness could only have been accomplished by Jesus because of his uniquely divine nature, but the mystics would disagree. They would say that everyone possesses this capability, but most people aren't awake enough to know it, like a bird that doesn't know what its wings are for, or how to use them. As the Australian band INXS said:

> *I told you that we could fly*
> *Because we all have wings*
> *But some of us don't know why.*[10]

Alternatively, we have The Doors, who said:

> *You know that it would be untrue*
> *You know that I would be a liar*
> *If I was to say to you*
> *Girl, we couldn't get much higher.*[11]

In the Pink Floyd song *Learning To Fly* there is also a suggestion of vast, infinite (hyper)space, but of being unable to rise above the earth-bound dimension to this ineffable sphere — of remaining nailed to the cross, as it were. The song begins:

> *Into the distance, a ribbon of black*
> *Stretched to the point of no turning back*
> *A flight of fancy on a windswept field*
> *Standing alone my senses reel*
> *A fatal attraction is holding me fast*
> *How can I escape this irresistible grasp*
>
> *Can't keep my eyes from the circling skies*
> *Tongue-tied and twisted*
> *Just an earth-bound misfit, I...*

The ribbon which is "stretched to the point of no turning back" can be identified as a reference to hyperspace, like the cross in Dali's painting. The person in the song resolves to surmount his leaden-footedness, and to learn to use his hitherto unutilized subtle wings. These initial efforts, as momentous as the first steps of an infant, are described:

> *A soul in tension that's learning to fly*
> *Condition grounded but determined to try.*

The soul is in tension because it is still plagued by the distinctions and divisions of the corporeal world, but the all-important beginning has been made. Without this beginning, however unsteady or uncertain, no destination is ever reached. As the Tao Te Ching says: "The journey of a thousand *li*[12] starts from where one stands." Like the Eastern mystics, the soul-aviator of the song realizes that he will have to be the shaper of his own destiny and bring about his own redemption. Once he has mastered the spiritual techniques for this self-emancipation, his magnificent inner wings unfurl and beat powerfully, sending him soaring into the heady dimension beyond illusion and suffering, of which he says:

> *There's no sensation to compare with this*
> *Suspended animation, a state of bliss.*

The mention of suspended animation brings to mind the suspension of Christ above the dimension of mere mortals in Dali's painting. The soul that was in tension because of the conflicts and paradoxes of the earthly dimension has now reached hyperspace and has seen these paradoxes as being contained in the one hyperbody, and so is released from its bondage and suffering. It has shuffled off its mortal coil and become one with the sublime hyperbody itself.

The transformation of the physical, limited body into a transcendent and spiritual "diamond" or "lightning" body was also the aim of the ancient Chinese text *The Secret of the Golden Flower*. Jung, in his commentary on this alchemical text (which was translated by Richard Wilhelm), writes the following about the "diamond body" that is produced as a result of effecting the necessary transmutation of consciousness:

> It is, in fact, a change of feeling similar to that experienced by a father to whom a son has been born, a change known to us from the testimony of St. Paul: "Yet not I, but Christ liveth in me." The symbol "Christ" as "son .of man" is an analogous psychic experience of a higher spiritual being who is invisibly born in the individual, a pneumatic body which is to serve us as a future dwelling, a body which, as Paul says, is put on like a garment. . . It is, in a sense, the feeling that we have been "replaced," but without the connotation of having been "deposed."[13]

The *Hui Ming Ching*, which accompanied the *Golden Flower* text, describes how this diamond body is to be attained:

> *If thou wouldst complete the diamond body with no outflowing,*
> *Diligently heat the roots of consciousness and life.*
> *Kindle light in the blessed country close at hand,*
> *And there hidden, let thy true self always dwell.*

Here again we see that "heat," or intense effort, like the *tapas* of yoga, is necessary to rise above the mortal body, to unfurl the mystic wings of the soul and ascend to the "blessed country" — the hyper-space which contains all earthly bodies just as a cube contains each of the planes that make up its sides. This is the exalted vantage point, the realm of Brahman, from which one looks down on the lower world and realizes that all its forms are just different aspects of the one transcendent higher-dimensional reality.

However, while rigorous disciplining of the mind and body under the supervision of an enlightened master are undoubtedly necessary for a sustained and lasting vision of the divine radiance that pervades all, the highest insight sometimes appears in a fleeting moment to ordinary individuals in their everyday lives, in a flash of realization that they are one with everybody else. The veil of illusion is temporarily lifted and the truth is seen as stated in the Isa Upanishad: "Who sees all beings in his own Self, and his own Self in all beings, loses all fear." This proposition is best explained by the splendid Buddhist image of Indra's Net of Gems. This net is said to be a vast interconnected network of shining pearls or gems hanging over the palace of the god Indra, in which each gem reflects all the others and is similarly reflected in all the others. In the same way, each person in the world contains all others, and they in turn contain him.[14]

The profound realization of this interpenetration of one's own self and the self of all others can lead to extraordinary acts of empathy and altruism, such as when a person places his or her life in danger to save another, or when a soldier willingly sacrifices his life for his country or comrades. Here, the line dividing the individual (ego) and others (non-ego) is temporarily obliterated. The individual abandons his solipsistic self-absorption and realizes that he is identical with the person he is trying to save, and that their soul is one. This idea was taken up and pursued by Schopenhauer (who was greatly influenced by the Upanishads) when he wrote about how the suffering of another can touch him and move him to action to alleviate the other's distress as if it were his own:

> But this presupposes that to a certain extent I have identified myself with the other man, and in consequence the barrier between ego and non-ego is for the moment abolished; only then do the other man's affairs, his need, distress, and suffering, directly become my own. I no longer look at him as if he were something given to me by empirical

intuitive perception, as something strange and foreign, as a matter of indifference, as something entirely different from me. On the contrary, I share the suffering in him, in spite of the fact that his skin does not enclose my nerves. Only in this way can his woe, his distress, become a motive for me; otherwise it can absolutely be only my own.[15]

And later in the same book Schopenhauer has this to say about the nature of charitable actions and disinterested help:

> It is practical mysticism insofar as it ultimately springs from the same knowledge that constitutes the essence of all mysticism proper. In no other way can it be truly explained. That a man gives alms without having, even remotely, any other object than that of lessening the want that oppresses another, is possible only insofar as he recognizes that it is his own self which now appears before him in that doleful and dejected form, and hence that he recognizes again his own inner being-in-itself in the phenomenal appearance of another.

Love as Mystical Union

If the suffering and distress of strangers can move us to such an extent that the supreme paradox of life is briefly resolved and the bonds of ignorance temporarily loosened, how much more should that be the case with romantic love and intimacy, since it is a much more intense and heightened experience of the union of two (seemingly) disparate souls. Indeed, Jung said of love and sexual union:

> Normal sex life, as a shared experience with apparently similar aims, further strengthens the feeling of unity and identity. This state is described as one of complete harmony, and is extolled as a great happiness ("one heart and one soul") — not without good reason, since the return to that original condition of unconscious oneness is like a return to childhood. Hence the childish gestures of all lovers. Even more is it a return to the mother's womb, into the teeming depths of an as yet unconscious creativity. It is, in truth, a genuine and incon-

testable experience of the Divine, whose transcendent force obliter-ates and consumes everything individual.[16]

With this in mind, we now have a better appreciation of the deeper meaning when John Lennon says, in *Dear Yoko*:

After all is really said and done
The two of us are really one.

And if we realize that the experience of love is a return to the origi-nal state of the unconscious, where time and space do not exist as sepa-rate categories, then the following line in Paul McCartney's *Maybe I'm Amazed* also achieves greater clarity: "Baby, I'm amazed at the way you pulled me out of time."

So, if love and compassion lead to an epiphany of transcendent knowledge, and thus nullify the action of *Maya*, then universal love for all creation can be seen to be the highest form of wisdom and the true path to liberation. This was the path prescribed by the Buddha as *ka-runa*, or compassion and empathy for all that lives. In the song *Across The Universe*, The Beatles gave a wonderful definition of *karuna*: "Limitless undying love which shines around me like a millions suns."

In the song *Mind Games*, Lennon offers his solution to the overcom-ing of *Maya* as: "Love is the answer." Love in this context surely means an all-pervading love for life and all that lives, and such an all-encompassing love breaks down the barriers between individuals as separate entities. Taken to its logical conclusion, *karuna* leads to a clear understanding that there is only one universal consciousness of which everyone and everything is an indistinguishable part, the description of which is beyond the scope of language, since language divides every-thing into subject and object and therefore perpetuates the erroneous subject-object split.

According to Alan Watts, love includes in its fold not just sexual relations and intimacy between men and women but all forms of inter-action and mutual exchange, such as between organism and environ-ment, and it also encompasses all so-called opposites. He writes:

It is hardly stretching a metaphor to use the word "love" for intimate relationships beyond those between human organisms. In those states of consciousness called "mystical" we have, I believe, a sudden slip into an inverse or obverse of the view of the world given in our divisive language forms. Where this slip is not, as in schizophrenia, a tortured withdrawal from conflict, the change of consciousness again and again brings the overwhelming impression that the world is a system of love. Everything fits into place in an indescribably harmony — indescribable because paradoxical in the terms which our language provides.[17]

Perhaps the last word on the subject belongs to Peter Gabriel, who in his song *In Your Eyes* describes the recognition of his universal self in the eyes of a beloved. All religion, all art, all passion, the search for his very soul, melt away and coalesce in those eyes:

In your eyes
The light the heat
In your eyes
I am complete
In your eyes
I see the doorway to a thousand churches
In your eyes
The resolution of all the fruitless searches.

The Roots of Discord

Freedom from the hoax played on us by *Maya* can only be won by dissolving the borders that separate individuals and keep them indifferent from each other and the world, and by embracing all of creation as one indivisible soul. Conversely, the true cause of conflict, suffering and discord can be understood to lie in the artificial divisions created in the minds of men and women taking literally the effusion of forms and different categories of perception created by their critical and analyzing consciousness.

It has long been recognized by war propagandists and militant jingoists that if human beings are to be goaded into fighting wars, killing each other, and performing unspeakable acts of torture and barbarism, it is necessary to subvert the underlying (though consciously unrealized) intimation of the oneness of all beings. This is done by dehumanizing and distancing the designated enemy, and thus removing any sense of identification that may be felt with him, and which may give rise to undesirable feelings of pity or remorse. It is to be noted that this is the antithesis of the intuitive insights afforded by feelings of love and empathy, as elucidated by Schopenhauer and Jung above. The psychologist Erich Fromm, who has studied human destructiveness in depth, explains:

> Another way of making the other a "nonperson" is cutting all affective bonds with him. This occurs as a permanent state of mind in certain severe pathological cases, but it can also occur transitorily in one who is not sick. It does not make any difference if the object of one's aggression is a stranger or a close relative or a friend; what happens is that the aggressor cuts the other person off emotionally and "freezes" him. The other ceases to be experienced as human and becomes a "thing — over there." Under these circumstances there are no inhibitions against even the most severe forms of destructiveness.[18]

Any inflammation of feelings of enmity or hatred are bound to blind people to inner truth because their object is always external, and hatred is a form of bondage to its object. Tension, strife, and conflict only arise because of the clash between opposing, irreconcilable forces. Once it is comprehended that all dichotomies are in fact mutually inclusive, then these antagonistic forces collapse and merge together, polarities cease to exist, and no ground remains where rivalries and hatreds can gain a foothold.

Jimi Hendrix, one of the most creative and pioneering musicians in all of contemporary music, sang the following words in *Machine Gun*, a song that he regularly played live to the accompaniment of the sounds of his guitar making the amplifier scream in simulation of a battlefield in Vietnam and the agonized wails of the dying wounded:

Evil men make me kill you
Evil men make you kill me
Evil men make me kill you
Even though we're only families apart

The failure lies in not being aware of our deep-rooted kinship with each other and of our common origins in pre-history. The ageless voice of humanity calls out to us to break down the barriers we have created that keep us apart and prevent us from establishing our true identity with all that was, is, and shall ever be. Once the callous indifference to the suffering of other living beings is replaced by the warm, all-embracing *karuna* of the Buddha, then the wisdom dawns that all divisiveness is based on a tragic perceptual error and has no reality outside the human mind.

The process by which antagonisms arise in the mind, and then take over, can be outlined as follows. All perceived slights and injustices go towards building up the storehouse of memories within each person, and on the basis of this storehouse future actions are determined. Furthermore, what constitutes an injustice or an offence is different in each case, for people have varying levels of tolerance based on personal and culturally-conditioned factors. Therefore, the different memories, life experiences, and social environments of individuals cause different responses to be elicited to the same set of external conditions, and therefore all aggression and hostility is no more than a form of response that is conditioned by memory and instilled values. Only by clearing this tangled heap of archaic prejudices, resentments, and grudges that clutter and stifle the mind can a person become suffused with *karuna* and know the timeless truth that will set him free. No clearer and more direct assertion of this fact can be found than the following lyrics from the song *Fill Your Heart* on David Bowie's *Hunky Dory* album:

Fill your heart with love today
Don't play the game of time
Things that happened in the past
Only happened in your mind

Only in your mind
Forget your mind
And you'll be free.

Transforming Perception

The root of the problem of existence lies in the fact that the ordinary understanding of the human situation is founded on inappropriate models of thought, cognition, and experience. Therefore, a radical change and readjustment of consciousness and the way of looking at oneself and the world is needed if man is to extricate himself from the web of illusions he has spun all around him, and in which all are entangled. As the famous quotation goes: "Oh, what a tangled web we weave, when first we practice to deceive!"[19] To penetrate beyond the layers upon layers of lies and deception that are heaped upon us from the moment of our birth is to reach the fulfillment of the Socratic edict: "Know thyself" (which the Eastern thinkers would in all likelihood have preferred to reformulate slightly, as, "Know thy *real and undifferentiated self*"). This self can be likened to a flame burning within a lamp that has become covered with mud and dirt, and so the sacred flame is hidden. Only by cleaning the surface of the lamp, that is, by adjusting and recalibrating the misaligned patterns of mental functioning, can the clear, bright inner light shine through and be seen.

All forms and all relations must be seen in a new light, free from the false assumptions and associations of the past, which we have created for ourselves and which society has thrust upon us. All that has been learned must be unlearned. We are used to grasping, clinging, and acquiring; we must instead learn to open ourselves to the true meaning of every leaf, every flower, every stone, stripped bare of the confounding layers that our mental process imposes on it. William Blake best described the nature of this perceptual acuity, once it is acquired:

To see a world in a grain of sand
And a heaven in a wild flower
Hold infinity in the palm of your hand
And eternity in an hour.[20]

Becoming completely open and receptive to the Divine can be likened to the action of a lightning rod, a conduit that is able to capture and utilize the field of radiant energy that surrounds and binds everything. Otherwise, the wondrous beauty that sparkles all around simply passes by unnoticed and disregarded, like the bag of gold at the doorstep of Shiva's devotee.

John Lennon describes the psychological transformation that must be effected before the awakening and channeling of internal cosmic energies can take place:

> *Yes is the answer, and you know that for sure*
> *Yes is surrender*
> *You got to let it, you got to let it go.*[21]

The answer lies in affirming our true nature as infinite bliss, and overcoming the psychological mechanisms that create obstructions and resistances to our knowledge of this fundamental and liberating fact. This can only be done by releasing our tenacious grip on the self-image created by our rational, analyzing mind — a psychic unclenching and surrender to our higher self. Hence the ancient Chinese saying: "To yield is to be preserved whole."[22]

It is this desire to go beyond the artificial boundaries and conceptual constructs of the mind that Lennon sang about in *Imagine*; and in the song *Yer Blues* on The Beatles' *White Album*[23] he sang:

> *My mother was of the sky*
> *My father was of the earth*
> *But I am of the universe*
> *And you know what it's worth*

By transcending the opposites of heaven and earth, and all such earthly pairs of opposites, by regarding all that we perceive around us as issuing forth from, and returning to, the one omnipresent Soul, comes the awareness that the true essence of the innermost self, which is hidden from the senses, is identical with the essence of the universe. Only by knowing that the central axis of our individual being is coincident with the central axis of the world (*axis mundi*) can we overcome our differences and achieve true harmony between all.

To account for these seemingly non-intuitive facts, there must ex-ist a universal energy source which permeates and animates all that lives, and from which all forms and thought originate. Of this transcen-dent, ever-flowing source the Katha Upanishad says:

> This by which we perceive colours and sounds, perfumes and kisses of love; by which alone we attain knowledge; by which verily we can be conscious of anything: This in truth is That.

. Thus, out of the Great Void, the immanent energy source, individ-ual consciousness emerges like a spark from the cosmic flame. It plays its role in the great drama of human existence, during which period it derives its energy and sustenance from the creative power of the void, and then returns once more to it at the drama's close. What the great seers recognized is that this void is the hub from which all life and the forms of the world spring forth, and that the infinite reserve of energy which supplies us, supplies also the entire universe. This idea is echoed in the following lines from the Police song, *Invisible Sun*:

> *There has to be an invisible sun*
> *It gives its heat to everyone.*

In the movie *Network*, the news anchor Howard Beale has a pro-phetic vision in his sleep one night, and the next morning he goes on public television to proclaim the truth he received, and which has now been made clear to him by a radical transformation of his conscious-ness. His description of his awakening is initially taken by his friend, Max, as resulting from a hallucination or even a mental breakdown, but there is no denying its extreme proximity to the central tenets of East-ern thought, which Beale even referred to directly when describing his vision, as follows:

> This is not a psychotic episode! This is a cleansing moment of clarity. I'm imbued, Max, I'm imbued with some special spirit. It's not a reli-gious feeling at all. It's a shocking eruption of great electrical energy. I

feel vivid flashings, as if suddenly I've been plugged into some great electromagnetic field. I feel connected to all living things — flowers, birds, all the animals of the world. And even to some great unseen living force — what I think the Hindus call prana. It is not a break-down! I've never felt more orderly in my life. It is a shattering and beautiful sensation. It is the exalted flow of the space-time contin-uum, save that it is spaceless and timeless. Such loveliness! I feel on the verge of some great ultimate truth.

To fully understand and appreciate these initially inscrutable and alien ideas, which apparently stand in direct contrast to what our eve-ryday experience tells us, requires unlearning all the fictions and half-truths we have grown up with, a reawakening of consciousness to see the world and its inhabitants afresh, not as split-off egos separated from the external world and defined by some abstract entity within their skin but as mutually dependent organisms that define and com-plement each other. This view of the universe, however, is in complete dissonance with the traditional Western rationalistic and scientific view that posits each individual as an insignificant little creature living on an inconsequential planet in the backwaters of the universe. Even in Western religion each man is regarded as merely one sheep in a multi-tudinous flock, to be guided and led by the Good Shepherd. Therefore, when a person professes mystical ideas or experiences of transcendent unity, he is saying things that are beyond the pale of consensus opinion, and thus he is automatically regarded as a crank or a psychotic.

It has been drummed into our heads from infancy that we stand apart from each other and our environment, and that we need to over-power and conquer nature to be really free, whereas the truth is that organism and nature form part of an interlocking whole and we cannot speak about one without speaking also of the other. This idea is per-haps best explained by referring to certain drawings by M. C. Escher, where the figures in the drawings are not clear-cut and distinct objects, but instead the boundary of each figure defines and shapes the bounda-ries of the others.[24] It is not possible to describe any one figure without also describing the figures surrounding it. This is how the world and the individual are also to be understood.

So, it does not make sense to talk about what is inside an organism and what is outside it, for they are both two sides of the same coin and no attempt should be made to cleave them apart. Furthermore, and more radically, the outside world is to be seen as simply a function or a state of the sense organs and nervous system of the organism that is perceiving it. When a person sees a tree or feels a rock, these are changes in the states of the nervous system effected by the eyes and fingers, and hence are inside the person and not outside. The observer and the observed thing are one and the same. The confusion arises only when the ego enters into the picture, as a detached entity inside one's head that thinks it is doing the observing and feeling and which causes one to say "I am seeing" and "I am touching." It is this very ego which is the agent of *Maya*. Alan Watts writes:

> One of the important physical facts that socialization represses is that all our sensory experiences are states of the nervous system. The field of vision, which we take to be outside the organism, is in fact inside it because it is a translation of the external world into the form of the eye and the optical nerves. What we see is therefore a state of the organism, a state of ourselves. Yet to say even this is to say too much. There is not the external world, and then the state of the nervous system, and then something which sees that state. The seeing is precisely that particular state of the nervous system, a state which for that moment is an integral part of the organism.[25]

So, if it was not clear before, the meaning of the lines below sung by The Beatles now reveals itself:

> *Your inside is out and your outside is in*
> *Your outside is in and your inside is out.*[26]

All of these insights attest to the fact that the only reality is the One Mind, *dharmakaya*, and nothing more. The abundant and swarming images of life, which make so strong an impression on consciousness, are wholly a product of the psyche; a psyche which is, furthermore, universal.

Jung arrived at a similar idea via his notion of the *subjective factor*, which is closely linked to the functioning of apperception. Apperception is the process by which an object or concept is compared to an already in-place psychic content, by which means it is comprehended by consciousness. This is a two-step process. First, the object is perceived. Then it is assimilated to a pre-existing pattern in the mind by means of which it is comprehended and transformed into psychic images. The exact form that these images take depends on the subjective factor, the unconscious disposition of the psyche. Thus, for example, sound is actually vibrations in the air and it is the subjective factor which translates the vibrations into sounds. Similarly, wavelengths of light are perceived as colors; the principle of existence is believed to be "God," "matter," or "energy." Sounds, colors, and matter are not absolute, objective facts, but *a priori* concepts or structures within the psyche, according to which the phenomena of the universe are shaped, molded, and then presented to the conscious mind. The quality, strength, and vividness of the ensuing mental impression depend on the subjective factor.

The laws of apperception are immutable, although the images and concepts which are the results of its work vary according to circumstance. To quote Jung directly:

> Every new representation, be it a perception or a spontaneous thought, arouses associations which derive from the storehouse of memory. These leap immediately into consciousness, producing the complex picture of an "impression," though this is already a sort of interpretation . . .

> Existence is as we see and understand it.[27] There are innumerable things that can be seen, felt, and understood in a great variety of ways. Quite apart from merely personal prejudices, the psyche assimilates external facts in its own way, which is based ultimately upon the laws or patterns of apperception. These laws do not change, although different ages or different parts of the world call them by different names. On a primitive level people are afraid of witches; on the modern level we are apprehensively aware of microbes. There everybody believes in ghosts, here everybody believes in vitamins. Once upon a time men were possessed by devils, now they are not less obsessed by ideas, and so on.[28]

The series of events can be roughly imagined as follows. Every experience and sensation, as soon as it is felt, is immediately dragged down into the unconscious. There it is matched against a grid of instinctual patterns and assimilated with any number of them, depending on the subjective factor. Only then, after it has been re-forged, is the assimilated content cast onto the conscious realm, where it is now registered as a feeling, impression, or thought.

Within the unconscious mind there is a vast matrix of patterns and motifs; they are its structural and defining elements, and they, via apperception, determine the images and concepts presented to the conscious mind.[29] The plurality of forms and categories of thought can thus be seen to originate from this deeply embedded psychic matrix, which is now recognizable as the real birthplace of the hitherto external gods, demons, and supernatural forces. The action of apperception is identical to that of *Maya*, in that it takes real aspects of the world and then modifies them (according to the subjective factor) before they reach conscious realization.

By understanding this process, one comes to terms with the eternal patterns of psychic functioning, and so can attenuate the impact of any interposed alteration in the path from an objective reality to the subjective perception of it. Then it finally can be seen that the appearance of the world depends entirely on one's mental condition, and that as long as the mind remains clouded or perturbed, the world becomes proportionately enigmatic and unknowable. Like Daedalus's labyrinth, the phenomenal world is our own creation, and as long as we remain trapped inside it we are forced to operate within the narrow confines of its passageways.

Kundalini — Ascent of the Serpent Power

The classic symbolic depiction of the awakening self is that employed by kundalini yoga. Kundalini represents a latent reserve of infinite energy inherent within every individual, and is depicted as a serpent lying coiled at the base of the spine. In most individuals this serpent lies dormant and languid, but the yogic masters are able to awaken it, and once aroused it rises up and pierces in turn the seven ascending energy centers (*chakras*) of the body located along the spinal column, each higher *chakra* representing a correspondingly higher state of consciousness. Perfect illumination is obtained when finally the highest *chakra*, at the crown of the head, is reached.[30]

It is worthwhile to elaborate further on this symbolism, for it is extraordinarily potent. First, let us consider the use of the serpent to represent latent cosmic energy. As it lies inert or glides along the ground, the serpent remains in the lower realm of the earth. It is confined to an almost two-dimensional existence, seeing only that which is closest to the surface. This is the condition of those trapped in the lower *chakras*, who are slaves to the lower passions and who believe only in what their senses convey to them; in short, it is the condition of those who are ensnared in the web of *Maya* and are taken in by superficial appearances. But when the serpent slowly lifts its head it sees the world increasingly in its three-dimensional aspect, and so the awakening of kundalini energy is likened to the rising up of a once-slumbering serpent through the higher *chakras*. What was hidden is now revealed to the inner eye in an upward, uplifting process of growth and awareness, as one by one the potential energy of each *chakra* is activated.

The heightened perception now achieved is seen as a spiritual rebirth, and therefore the serpent serves as an appropriate symbol for it, since it regularly sloughs off its skin and is thus "reborn." When the kundalini serpent stands fully erect, with its head in the highest heavens and its tail grounded fully in the deepest earth, then mind and body, spirit and matter, consciousness and unconscious are perfectly integrated, and the result is rapturous illumination.

The song *The End*, by The Doors, contains the following lines which clearly have a strong affinity with the kundalini imagery:

> *Ride the snake, ride the snake*
> *To the lake, the ancient lake, baby*
> *The snake is long, seven miles*
> *Ride the snake*
> *He's old, and his skin is cold.*

The obvious similarities require little comment. The snake is the serpent power of kundalini, and he is old because the energy he personifies is primal and cosmic, the infinite expanse of life-force concentrated and condensed within every single individual. Riding the snake refers to releasing and harnessing the full potential of kundalini, and the seven miles correspond to the seven *chakras.*

To fully understand the meaning of the "ancient lake," however, it is necessary to be somewhat familiar with the second *chakra* of the series. A brief explanation of the *chakras* is therefore in order, and where there are parallels with song lyrics, these will be brought to light in the relevant places. Of course, in this discussion we can only scratch the surface of this highly complex, recondite, and ancient mystical philosophy.[31]

Each *chakra* is visualized as being located at a particular region of the body along the spinal column, and usually has associated with it an elemental substance, an animal, and a unique set of symbols to help reveal its meaning. The lowest *chakra,* located in the region of the perineum, is called *muladhara.* It holds the root of all things, and its element is the Earth. It is the foundation of the world, and its symbol is the elephant, which supports the world on its back. It is the world of three-dimensional space and linear time. It also represents being engaged in the affairs, activities, and relationships of life in its mundane aspect. One pursues pleasures, acquires and hoards wealth, and performs the duties that society and family life demand. The lines below, by The Doors, typify this solidly grounded but uninspiring conscious state, and provide an inkling of something greater and more meaningful lying beyond it, waiting to be discovered — namely, the higher *chakras:*

> *We chased our pleasures here*
> *Dug our treasures there*
> *But can you still recall the time we cried*
> *Break on through to the other side.*[32]

An even more apt description of *muladhara* consciousness is Bob Dylan's whirlwind tour of the life, influences, and priorities of the average individual:

Get born, keep warm
Short pants, romance
Learn to dance, get dressed, get blessed
Try to be a success
Please her, please him
Buy gifts, don't steal, don't lift
Twenty years of schooling
And they put you on the day shift
Look out kid
They keep it all hid.[33]

The next *chakra* in the series is the *svadisthana chakra*, located in the genital region. Its element is Water and it represents the unconscious, or the unknown within us.[34] Entering this *chakra* means leaving behind the world of the commonplace and entering the world of the uncon-scious. The animal associated with this center is the *makara*, the levia-than or sea monster. It embodies the dangers inherent in entering this dark and forbidding zone, where the adventurer is devoured by the monster and then resurrected to continue his journey. The mythologi-cal depiction of entering into this chthonic realm is the descent into the cave or underworld, or the plunge into deep, dark waters. We shall have more to say about this imagery later, but for now we can draw a parallel between the "ancient lake" of The Doors' *The End* mentioned above, and the abyssal waters of the *svadisthana chakra*. The ancient lake is universal consciousness, teeming with ancient occult powers and timeless images, whose mysterious energies have to be assimilated; oth-erwise, they overwhelm the mind and shatter it to pieces.

After emerging from *svadisthana*, the next *chakra* we encounter is the *manipura chakra*, in the region of the navel. The element here is Fire, and in it one is born into a new existence after having been swallowed by the *makara* in the primordial ocean of *svadisthana*. This is the center of heightened desire, where the passions and senses are aflame. The ani-mal of this *chakra* is the ram — a sacrificial animal — and so the sym-bols considered in their entirety can be taken to mean that the passions and senses are increased in intensity after the baptism by water, and they must be cast into the sacrificial fire, surrendered to a higher goal. Only by creating a bonfire of the lower urges and impulses does man clear the way to his higher nature, after all obstacles and barriers to his spiritual advancement have been consumed in the great conflagration. Those who fail to do this are sentenced to forever blindly groping around in the dank prison of banality. Miss your chance to light the fateful spark, and you do yourself irretrievable harm, as the following lyrics by The Doors imply:

The time to hesitate is through
No time to wallow in the mire
Try now we can only lose
And our love become a funeral pyre
Come on baby, light my fire
Come on baby, light my fire
Try to set the night on fire.[35]

Fire is the great purifier and cleanser, and so after the *manipura chakra* we come upon the subtle and refined *anahata chakra*, situated at the level of the heart. This is the first center that concerns itself with higher and sublimated human (as opposed to animal) aims and drives, such as art, religion and philosophy. Its element is Air, or Wind, which wafts the spirit into the higher plane above earth-bound existence. In this *chakra* one withdraws from the emotions, and is no longer identical with them. Once the bestial passions are subdued, the first glimpse of the self in its entirety appears, not just that which is identified with the body and the personal mind. William Blake describes on a cosmic scale the entry to the sublime *anahata* from the fire of *manipura*:

The ancient tradition that the world will be consumed in fire at the end of six thousand years is true, as I have heard from Hell.

For the cherub with his flaming sword is hereby commanded to leave his guard at the tree of life, and when he does, the whole creation will be consumed, and appear infinite and holy, whereas it now appears finite and corrupt.

This will come to pass by an improvement of sensual enjoyment.

But first, the notion that man has a body distinct from his soul, is to be expunged.[36]

The gazelle is the animal linked with the *anahata chakra*. It is extremely light on its feet, shy and elusive. Although it is in contact with the earth, when in flight it has an almost bird-like quality, jumping in great leaps and bounds over the ground, almost defying gravity. Therefore, it serves as an apt symbol for the light and airy quality of the psychical substance, which is just beginning to be discerned from the heavy, corporeal earth. However, like the gazelle, the self proves to be very elusive and higher centers will have to be reached before it is firmly grasped.

The fifth in the series is the *visuddha chakra*, at the level of the neck, whose element is Ether. It is to be noted that the elements become progressively more volatile and rarefied the higher up the *chakras* we go. First earth, then water, then fire, then air, and now the completely intangible ether. Reaching this *chakra* signifies a sphere of total abstraction, far beyond the empirical world, where one realizes that matter is but a psychical concept. It is a climbing up from the *saguna* world of gross substance to the *nirguna* world of subtle essence within the mind. The psyche and the mind become the only realities, and, recalling the words of Blake, the notion that man has a body distinct from his soul is expunged.

In the previous *chakra*, the *anahata*, thought and feeling were identical with specific objects or people in the external world. In *visuddha* one realizes that the inner world determines, or projects, the outer, which is therefore only a reflection of the psyche. In this *chakra* the subjective experience and psychic condition are of prime importance, and so happiness and joy are not dependent on the external world. There is a constant flow of pulsing energy which illumines the mind and thrills the body, regardless of the current circumstances of life.

It is interesting to note that *visuddha*, like the root *muladhara chakra*, is also represented by the elephant. However, in *muladhara* it was supporting the *saguna* world, whereas here it is supporting the *nirguna*. The power of the elephant is now lent to psychical, as opposed to physical, realities, which the intellect would ordinarily dismiss as mere abstractions. In *visuddha*, subjective mental concepts are invested with the same degree of reality as objective ones. In degenerate cases this can lead to absurdities, such as belief in trolls, pixies, and the tooth fairy. In the sublime case, the elephant lends its strength to a genuine and moving experience of the world as an extension of the self.

The *ajna chakra*, centered between the eyebrows, is the penultimate *chakra* in the series, and has no element or animal associated with it. In *visuddha*, psychic reality was still opposed to physical reality, and so the elephant was needed to maintain it. In *ajna*, however, there is nothing but psyche and nothing to sustain, so no element or animal is required because everything disappears into the self. Consciousness is extended to encompass each every facet of the world. The mystic eye and ear are fully open and receptive, and all delusion is dispelled. The following lyrics, by The Beatles, describe beautifully this supremely advanced conscious state:

> *Pools of sorrow, waves of joy*
> *Are drifting through my opened mind*
> *Possessing and caressing me*

> *Images of broken light which dance before me*
> *Like a million eyes*
> *They call me on and on across the universe.*[37]

Even though all contrapositions are reconciled in the *ajna chakra*, one last duality remains — that between psyche and non-psyche, self and non-self. Although the ego disappears completely and there is nothing but mind, there also exists a non-mind (or God) with which one has to ultimately unite, and so one hurdle remains to be crossed.

This last barrier is finally broken down when the *sahasrara chakra*, the thousand-petaled lotus *chakra* at the crown of the head, is reached and the self merges into Brahman, the invisible heart of all that is. There are no more categories of thought or feeling, no God, no subject, no object, and no differentiation — only Brahman. This is the unsurpassed and most exalted state of Nirvana, achieved by perhaps a handful of souls in the entire course of human history.

Footnotes

1. C.G. Jung, *Commentary on "The Secret of the Golden Flower."*
2. In *Myths and Symbols in Indian Art and Civilization,* Heinrich Zimmer explains the meaning of the holy syllable 'OM', or 'AUM':

> This mystical utterance ("aye," "amen") stemming from the sacred language of Vedic praise and incantation, is understood as an expression and affirmation of the totality of creation. A — is the state of waking consciousness, together with its world of gross experience. U — is the state of dreaming consciousness, together with its experience of the subtle shapes of dream. M — is the state of dreamless sleep, the natural condition of quiescent, undifferentiated consciousness, wherein every experience is dissolved into a blissful non-experience, a mass of potential consciousness. The Silence following the pronunciation of the three, A, U, and M, is the ultimate unmanifest, wherein perfected supraconsciousness totally reflects and merges with the pure, transcendental essence of Divine Reality — Brahman is experienced as Atman, the Self. AUM, therefore, together with its surrounding silence, is a soundsymbol of the whole of consciousness-existence, and at the same time its willing affirmation.

3. Freud's therapeutic method of free-association attempted to capture the contents of a patient's unconscious before they had been thus "sicklied o'er".
4. Fritjof Capra, *The Tao of Physics.*
5. Much of the following discussion on hyperbodies is based on the article *The 'Self' as Hyperbody — Nested Realities and the 'Fourth Dimension'* by John Fudjack and Patricia Dinkelaker.
6. More specifically, a person living in n dimensions can visualize only a projection of a hyperbody in $n+1$ dimensions.
7. See Illustration 4.
8. The mathematics that is used to obtain these three-dimensional projections of hyperbodies is obviously completely beyond the scope of this book.
9. This is also the first of the Buddha's Four Noble Truths. (See Chapter 1, Footnote 12)
10. INXS, *Never Tear Us Apart.*
11. The Doors, *Light My Fire.*
12. A *li* is about a third of a mile.
13. C. G. Jung, *Commentary on "The Secret of the Golden Flower."*
14. A modern analogy can be drawn with the World Wide Web, a global net-

work consisting of millions of nodes linked by communication lines such that any mode is accessible by any other. The feeling that people often get while plugged in to the World Wide Web is, "We're all connected!," a feeling which has definite mystical resonance.

15. Schopenhauer, *On the Basis of Morality*.

16. C. G. Jung, *The Development of Personality*.

17. Alan Watts, *Psychotherapy East and West*.

18. Erich Fromm, *The Anatomy of Human Destructiveness*.

19. Walter Scott, *Marmion Canto 6, Stanza 17*.

20. William Blake, *Auguries of Innocence*.

21. John Lennon, *Mind Games*.

22. *Tao Te Ching*.

23. The album is not formally titled, but this is how it is popularly known.

24. See Illustration 5.

25. Alan Watts, *Psychotherapy East and West*.

26. The Beatles, *Everybody's Got Something to Hide Except Me and My Monkey*.

27. That is, the ordinary experience of existence is based on subjective rather than objective factors.

28. C. G. Jung, *Psychological Commentary on "The Tibetan Book of the Great Liberation."*

29. In Jung's terminology, the structural elements are the archetypes. The function of apperception can be likened to that of projection. See Chapter 6 for a more detailed discussion of projection, archetypes, and other related terms.

30. See Illustration 6.

31. The following discussion of kundalini and the chakras is based largely on the book *The Psychology of Kundalini Yoga: Notes of the seminar given in 1932 by C. G. Jung*.

32. The Doors, *Break On Through*.

33. Bob Dylan, *Subterranean Homesick Blues*.

34. Water almost always represents the unconscious in mythological and religious symbolism.

35. The Doors, *Light My Fire*

36. William Blake, *The Marriage of Heaven and Hell*.

37. The Beatles, *Across The Universe*.

CHAPTER 4

THE MYSTICAL PERSPECTIVE

The Original State of Mind

The intractable confusion and perplexity that modern man finds himself confronting is neither the first, nor the natural, order of things. The original state of the mind of man, such as existed at the dawn of the human race and human consciousness in the early mists of time, was one of existence wholly and completely in the unconscious, where the oneness of all things and the unity of opposites discussed above were directly experienced as a living reality. In the same way, each new entrant to the planet earth is also initially immersed in this state of unconscious existence, and the subsequent development of the ego and consciousness in the child parallels the development of these in the human race as a whole. Thus the growing baby is essentially reliving the evolutionary stages of the mind of his/her race from its earliest beginnings.[1]

The mind of the primitive man is similarly at a rudimentary stage of conscious development, and so it also remains submerged in the unconscious to a greater or lesser extent because of an insufficient strengthening of its rational and analytical faculties. Therefore, since primitive cultures and infants alike lack a highly developed and specialized consciousness, which is responsible for the feeling that one is a clearly demarcated and autonomous personality, the nature of life and existence as experienced by them both is one of *participation mystique*[2] with the world at large. They perceive of the world as an indivisible whole, which by its very nature engulfs and absorbs everything individual.

However, because consciousness is absent or at best hopelessly weak at this point, there is no sense of identity or self for them to relate the phenomena of the world to, and so these phenomena are seen as being internal to, and inseparable from, the pre-conscious individual. In short, there is no distinction between the internal world of the psyche and the external world perceived by the senses. Of this incipient state of the mind, where ego and consciousness still exist only in a germinal form within the unconscious, Erich Neumann, a student of Jung and a pioneering psychologist in his own right, says:

> The world is experienced as all-embracing, and in it man experiences himself, as a self, sporadically and momentarily only. Just as the infantile ego, living this phase over again, feebly developed, easily tired, emerges like an island out of the ocean of the unconscious for moments only, and then sinks back again, so early man experiences the world. Small, feeble, and much given to sleep, i.e., for the most part unconscious, he swims about in his instincts like an animal. Enfolded and upborne by great Mother Nature, rocked in her arms, he is delivered over to her for good or ill. Nothing is himself; everything is world.[3]

Thus, the primitive man lives an existence in which he is wholly fused with the natural world and all its forms. He does not know where he begins and where the world ends. He is like the mystic, except that the mystic can relate himself to the transcendent mystery because he has achieved what the Japanese call *satori* — the conscious realization of the real nature of existence through a revelatory experience. The soul of the primitive is consumed by the cosmic fire and can see only the fire, whereas the soul of the mystic is purified by it and can see itself and all things in it.

In this original state, where the analyzing and categorizing consciousness is still inchoate, earthly opposites such as Good and Evil, Heaven and Earth, and relative designations in space such as Above and Below dissolve together inseparably. The wheel of time stands still, and spatial relationships have no relevance or meaning. This state of existence before the emergence of the ego and duality is described in the creation myths of many cultures as the original condition of the universe, where the creation of the universe and its infinity of forms is an allegory for the creation of consciousness and its manifold contents. Thus, the following verses from the Rig Veda, the most ancient and sacred of Hinduism's texts, dating back to around 1200-900 B.C., describe the universe prior to the creation of time and space, as well as the pre-ego state of the unconscious:

> There was neither non-existence nor existence then; there was neither the realm of space nor the sky which is beyond. What stirred? Where? In whose protection? Was there water, bottomlessly deep? There was neither death nor immortality then. There was no distinguishing sign of night nor of day. That one breathed, windless, by its own impulse. Other than that there was nothing beyond.[4]

And in the Maitri Upanishad it is written:

> In the beginning all was Brahman, ONE and infinite. He is beyond north and south, and east and west, and beyond what is above or below. His infinity is everywhere. In him there is neither above, nor across, nor below; and in him there is neither east nor west.

So, temporal designations such as Time, Night, and Day, and concrete spatial designations such as North, South, Above, and Below are to be considered as arbitrary limitations imposed by the human mind upon the unconscious, and upon the formless, timeless, and limitless soul-matter of the universe. That being so, the unconscious is best represented symbolically by the circle, the most perfect of figures. The circle is boundless, with no beginning or end, all points having a common center and hence being indistinguishable from one another — a perfect symbolic representation of the mystical experience. This explains the heavy usage of the circle in Buddhist mandalas, and its ubiquity in the imagery and art of religion and ritual.

The realization that conceiving of bodies and objects as being fixed in localized space is flawed, and the corresponding wisdom that the true nature of the world and the unconscious is better approximated by the symbolism of the circle, is given voice in the following Pink Floyd lyrics:

> Up and down
> And in the end there's only round and round and round.[5]

Emergence of Ego and Consciousness

The sublime existence in the original mental state of *participation mystique* is depicted allegorically in the Bible by the Garden of Eden, where man lived in blissful ignorance of distinctions, for he was forbidden by God to eat the fruit of the tree of knowledge of good and evil, which God had placed in the garden. This state of ignorance symbolizes perfect knowledge of the world and the self as beyond duality. The original sin of mankind, the Fall of Man, is represented as the tasting by Adam and Eve of the forbidden fruit, the acquiring of proscribed knowledge, and thereby ending forever the former state of perpetual bliss. What is acquired in this manner is the knowledge of opposites, of morality, of rational thought; and those who have thus sinned are cast out from heaven for their shameful folly. What is more, God placed at the east side of Eden cherubim and a flaming sword that turned every way, to prevent them from ever returning. Man is tainted by his sinful knowledge, banished from paradise, and deprived of the everlasting joy within it that he had once enjoyed. The Fall of Man, therefore, represents the emergence from the unconscious idyll of ego and consciousness, which now discriminate between objects, forms, and moral concepts, and therefore shatter the hitherto tranquil state of total contentment.

According to the Biblical story, another tree exists in Eden, the Tree of Life, which imparts divine knowledge of the everlasting soul, and of whose fruit Adam and Eve were not able to partake before being banished. Joseph Campbell has offered his interpretation that the Biblical symbol of Eden is to be understood as a heavenly state of bliss which lies unknown and untapped within us. The cherubim with the flaming sword stationed at the eastern gates of Eden to guard the Tree of Life represent the pairs of opposites on earth. Only by getting past the two gatekeepers, that is, by transcending all pairs of earthly oppo-sites,[6] can the Tree of Life be reached, knowledge of divine perfection re-attained, and the lost paradise found again.

A similar theme of transgression and punishment is related in the Greek myth of Prometheus. According the legend, Zeus forbids the gods to give fire to man, but Prometheus disobeys him, steals fire from Olympus, and brings it back with him to the world of mortals. Zeus, in his wrath, orders that Prometheus is to be chained to a rock in the Caucasus Mountains for the rest of eternity, with an eagle perpetually feasting on his liver. The liver is regenerated every day so that the wound is never allowed to heal, as the eagle is forever pecking at it. Zeus eventually sends Herakles to kill the eagle and free Prometheus, but requires that Prometheus always wear a ring made from the iron of the chain which bound him, and that the ring be set with a fragment of the rock to which he was tied. In this way, Zeus' original decree that Prometheus remain fastened to the rock still held good.[7]

Like most myths this can be, and has been, interpreted in many different ways. In the context with which we are dealing, we can at-tribute the source of Prometheus' guilt to the stealing of knowledge (fire) that was the exclusive property of the gods in high heaven and of which man, with all his failings and shortcomings, was deemed unwor-thy, lest he misuse it. Now, because of Prometheus' spectacular arro-gance, this knowledge was let loose in the world and man was con-demned to live under a burden that was far too great for him to bear. Therefore, Prometheus had to suffer the consequences of his sin by hav-ing his liver constantly plucked at. The liver, being a visceral organ in the lower regions of the body, represents instincts and passions, and having it constantly attacked by the eagle would make it hard to think of anything else. So, just as the chains keep him physically bound to the rock, the self-regenerating passions keep his mind bound to the lower instincts.

Just as mankind had to pay the price for the Original Sin of Adam and Eve by being banished from Heaven, so he had to pay the price for the fire-theft of Prometheus by being forever chained to his brutish passions. Through the compromise of the ring Prometheus was allowed to go free, but had to carry his chain and rock around with him wher-ever he went; so too man is doomed to always be tainted by some portion of his lower nature which corrupts him and prevents his complete liberation.[8] Bob Dylan alluded to both Original Sin and Promethean guilt in various places in his song, *Foot of Pride*, as the following extracts show:

> *It's like the earth just opened and swallowed him up*
> *He reached too high, was thrown back to the ground*

> *How to enter into the gates of paradise? No!*
> *How to carry a burden too heavy to be yours...*

The principle sin, the crushing burden, is that of hubris, of ego and pride, which have made their unwelcome appearance and unbalanced the spirit of equanimity and relatedness that existed between all things. Thus burdened, the dream of re-attaining admittance to Paradise looks impossibly remote. The sublime gets buried under a mountain of dross, and the most pressing task seems to be how to cope with this overwhelming guilt, this albatross around the neck. Once the sin of hubris is committed there is no turning back, and the ring of Prometheus can never be removed. As Bob Dylan said, in the same song:

> *Well, there ain't no going back*
> *When your foot of pride comes down*
> *Ain't no going back.*

In the movie *The Empire Strikes Back*, Luke Skywalker, the hero, is undergoing the training necessary to become a Jedi knight[9] under the instruction of Yoda, an enlightened master. In the early part of his training, Luke was successful in moving rocks and other small objects by telekinesis, simply by concentrating intensely on them. As the next level in his training, Yoda now asks Luke to lift his X-Wing fighter, a heavy spacecraft that has been completely submerged under water, in the same way that he moved the other objects. Luke says that Yoda is asking way too much, and protests that this totally different from moving small rocks around. Yoda's emphatic reply is: "No, no different!

Only different in your mind. You must unlearn what you have learned."
In other words, a return to the initial state of pristine purity is necessary, where forgotten potentialities can once again be resurrected and
reanimated.

In the original condition of the mind, there was no difference to be
seen between rock and ship, heavy and light, these being merely properties of gross matter (*prakriti*), which was simply an illusion and had
no existence apart from the mind that was perceiving it. With the advent of ego, self, and rationality, however, the Word was made Flesh,
the illusion was made real, and the subject-object split made permanent. Only by expanding the notion of the self as being present everywhere, and not as being immured in the wall of flesh that constitutes
the body, does the mind again return to its natural and uncorrupted
state, like the prodigal son returning to the family fold after a life of
profligate debauchery.

Unity of Opposites

The highest vision of the coming together of opposites and the removal of all perceptual distinctions is represented in the well-known
Chinese *yin-yang*[10] symbol, in which the opposites[11] are inextricably intertwined and form the two halves of an inseparable whole. Furthermore, and crucially, they each also contain some portion of each other,
so that one cannot exist in isolation, and in fact each half of the two
opposites is the causation of the other. Their true nature is that of the
intertwined unity, and they were originally experienced as such before
the differentiating ego and consciousness appeared on the scene and
pried them apart into separate categories in the mind. To emphasize or
focus on only one of the polarities, and to disregard the other half of the
composite whole, is to misunderstand its real nature.

In another scene in *The Empire Strikes Back*, Luke enters a cave where
he must confront the greatest evil, but where Yoda tells him his weapons will be useless. Once inside the cave, Luke comes across his arch-
enemy Darth Vader, the Lord of the Dark, and does battle with him. At
the conclusion of the battle he decapitates Vader, who always wears a
black face mask and helmet; but when he sees the severed head inside
the helmet, it is not Vader's, but his own. What this scene suggests is

that Luke's real enemy is himself, or rather his ego, his false sense of who he is. The real enemy is not external but internal, and he can only be vanquished by wisdom and understanding, not by physical weapons.

In another interpretation of the scene, what Luke is confronted with is the fact that his own self is present even in so evil a person as Vader, and that his error lies in defining himself in complete contradistinction to him. Later he discovers that Vader is, in fact, his father. Thus, good is contained in evil and vice versa, and one cannot exist without the other — precisely the insight that is conveyed by the yin-yang. The Tao Te Ching says:

> When the people of the world all know beauty as beauty, there arises the recognition of ugliness.

> When they all know the good as good, there arises the recognition of evil.

In light of this wisdom, it is easier to understand how the Tao Te Ching, the classic text of harmony and symbiosis between man and Nature, can contain chapters on military strategy, which seem startlingly incongruous among words espousing the virtues of tranquility, serenity and humility.

Thus also the Bhagavad Gita, which is essentially a treatise on the true nature of the soul and the universe, and which emphasizes detachment and withdrawal of the senses from the illusory world, is placed in the context of a devastating war which results in a blood bath. In it Krishna enjoins Arjuna, who is having grave doubts about participating in a fratricidal war, to partake in the battle but to keep in mind the overarching truth which he has just taught him, namely that the soul is eternal and the person who thinks that he can kill or be killed is mistaken. Only by recognizing and understanding the dual, paradoxical nature of the world can we transcend it. It may be noted that the discourse in the Gita takes place between the assembled ranks of the two opposing armies of good and evil, such that the master and disciple are equidistant from both ranks.[12] Furthermore, Krishna's counsel to Arjuna is:

86

Be in truth Eternal, beyond earthly opposites. Beyond gains and possessions, possess thine own soul.

The Web of Life/Gaia Theory

As consciousness and ego evolve and develop, the *participation mystique* and communion between the individual and the world gets progressively weaker, and the developing mind moves further and further
away from its original state. As consciousness gradually gains in
strength, the rationalizing and differentiating functions of the psyche
begin to dominate, and the world of unconscious images and potentialities recedes further into the dim recesses of the mind.

However, those who have re-established the link to the unconscious speak once more of the fusion of themselves with the natural
world, and the interconnectedness of all things. Their psyches are open
and receptive to the world in all its splendor, and they intuitively as-
cribe its contents as being internal to themselves. Furthermore, their
consciousness is considerably more developed than the primitive, and
so they have a means of relating themselves to the world of the unconscious and integrating it with their ego-awareness. As mentioned before, this is usually accomplished by means of symbols and images,
which serve as a connecting bridge between the two realms and guide
the individual along the path to the true self. The paradoxes and conflicts that had seemed inherent in the nature of the world suddenly resolve themselves and reveal the underlying clarity and simplicity. The
sensation is so moving that it leads to a revolution of consciousness, to
a radically different way of looking at the world, and this enlightened
outlook is often expressed metaphorically as a living connection between man and the world, between the inside and the outside.

The mind and self are now seen to reach out as far as one's environment extends and, given the thorough interconnectedness and interpenetration of all things, the entire world is to be understood as an extension of mind and body. There is, therefore, only a single, unified field
of organism and environment, and all life is an integral component of
this one great field.

Exactly this style of imagery was employed by Chief Seattle, the great American Indian chief, in his letter to the president of the United States just before the annexation of his land and the annihilation of his people. In the celebrated letter he spoke of the Web of Life — the intimate kinship that exists between man and nature. Here are a few excerpts from it:

> Every part of the earth is sacred to my people. Every shining pine needle, every sandy shore, every mist in the dark woods, every meadow, every humming insect. All are holy in the memory and experience of my people.

> We know the sap which courses through the trees as we know the blood that courses through our veins. We are part of the earth and it is part of us. The perfumed flowers are our sisters. The bear, the deer, the great eagle, these are our brothers. The rocky crests, the dew in the meadow, the body heat of the pony, and man all belong to the same family.

> . . . All things are connected like the blood that unites us all. Man did not weave the web of life, he is merely a strand in it. Whatever he does to the web, he does to himself.

> . . . One thing we know — there is only one God. No man, be he Red man or White man, can be apart. We ARE all brothers after all.

A similar communion and sense of mystical rapport with the natural world shines through in Bob Dylan's *Let Me Die In My Footsteps*, as exemplified by the following lines:

> *Let me drink from the waters where the mountain streams flood*
> *Let the smell of wildflowers flow free through my blood*
> *Let me sleep in your meadows with the green grassy leaves* .
> *Let me walk down the highway with my brother in peace.*

The Little River Band's *Cool Change* is also about identification with the natural elements of the earth — specifically, the enchanting, magical feeling of being alone on the vast sea, exulting in the sense of a deeply intimate bond with the endless expanse of water and all that is contained within it. The verse below is illustrative:

Well, I was born in the sign of water
And it's there that I feel my best
The albatross and the whales, they are my brothers
And it's kind of a special feeling when you're out on the sea alone
Staring at the full moon like a lover.

The conception of all units of life being a strand in one great inter-connected and interdependent tapestry has found confirmation in the modern age in the holistic Gaia[13] theory developed by James Lovelock, Lynn Margulis, and others. According to this theory, the earth is to be thought of not merely as an inert body upon whose surface living or-ganisms move around independently like ants crawling on a piece of stone, but is to be regarded instead as a living and intelligent organism, whose nature and composition is determined by the interactions be-tween it and all life forms existing on it.

According to Lovelock, the earth's atmosphere is created by the organisms living on it and is maintained by them at a level favorable for their optimum growth. That is, the planet is self-regulating. For exam-ple, about three billion years ago bacteria and algae began to remove carbon dioxide from the atmosphere and to produce oxygen as a waste product. This led to the point where, strange as it may sound today, the earth began to suffer from an excess of oxygen. This situation was only remedied by the advent of organisms that respired aerobically and con-sumed the oxygen. Thus, the cumulative actions of countless organ-isms, as a result of their life processes, were responsible for the change in atmosphere. This shows that the atmosphere of the earth and oceans is made amenable to the conditions of life by life itself, in contrast to the conventional approach that planetary conditions change of their own accord and that it is up to life to evolve and adapt itself to these changes.

Margulis added the interesting feature to the theory that the regu-lating interactions on earth often combine animate and inanimate com-ponents. An example of this is the carbon dioxide cycle. Usually the amount of carbon dioxide present in the atmosphere is kept at a constant because of the balance in the processes of respiration and photosynthesis in animals and plants. The respiration of animals produces carbon dioxide, which is consumed by the photosynthesis of plants, and so the net amount of the gas remains the same. However, certain disruptive events such as volcanic eruptions produce massive quantities of carbon dioxide, which greatly threaten the delicate balance because carbon dioxide is a greenhouse gas and has the effect of warming the planet. If left unchecked, it would make the earth too hot to be habitable.

This is where the phenomenon of rock weathering comes into play to remove excess quantities of carbon dioxide. In rock weathering, rainwater and carbon dioxide combine with rocks to form carbonates, a process which is greatly accelerated by the presence of soil bacteria. The carbonates are washed into the ocean, where microscopic algae use them to make shells. When the algae die, their shells fall to the bottom of the ocean and form limestone sediments there. The weight of the limestone causes it to sink beneath the earth's mantle, where it melts and is thus disposed of (although it may re-enter the atmosphere through another volcanic eruption).

The key to this whole series of events is that the soil bacteria are more active in high temperatures, and so the removal of carbon dioxide is accelerated when the planet is hot, and this has the effect of cooling it. In this whole cycle earth and life are in constant, intimate interaction, each influencing and modifying the other. In understanding how the planet works, it is impossible to discount the effect of life since it has a direct bearing on the constitution of the earth's crust, air, and water. Thus, soil, air, water, and all life contained within them are, in actuality, fused together into a single, intelligent organism, in opposition to the traditional view of the earth as simply an artifact or a finely-tuned but lifeless mechanism.

All this is also in glaring contrast to the widely-held anthropocentric view, which holds that the human species is the most important one and that all other life on the planet is subordinate to its interests and claims. This outdated and untenable view is now to be completely discredited. Instead, each life form is to be compared to a cell in a living body, where the living body is the earth. Anyone who violates any part of the earth harms the body of which he is an integral and dependent part, and so spells his own doom as well as that of all others. This is exactly what Chief Seattle was trying to make people understand, and what humanity has lost sight of today.

Reincarnation and Karma

The doctrines of reincarnation and karma are perhaps among the most well-known of the ideas to come out of India, and it is worthwhile discussing them here and trying to understand how these ideas also surface in the lyrics of contemporary songs.

Belief in reincarnation, or the transmigration of souls, is by no means unique to India, and has been widely held throughout the world among many different peoples. In its Indian version, the theory states that the soul of a man does not perish after he dies, and neither does it pass into a permanent state of existence in heaven, hell, or anywhere else. The soul, rather, takes on another body on earth, and when that dies it takes on another, and so on in an endless cycle of rebirths (*samsara*). In certain cases, one may still harbor memories or recollections from previous lives, and this is often used to account for feelings of *déjà vu* and certain forms of supra-sensory knowledge. This may explain why George Harrison claimed that the following Bob Dylan lyrics express perfectly the idea of reincarnation:

Look out kid
It's somethin' you did
God knows when
But you're doin' it again.[14]

The Beatles' song, *Helter Skelter,*[15] also contains suggestions of a relentless cosmic law of being, existing, perishing, and then recursion to the beginning again. The song starts:

When I get to the bottom, I go back to the top of the slide
Where I stop and I turn and I go for a ride
Then I get to the bottom and I see you again.[16]

If the slide is seen as an allegory for existence in this world, then these lyrics blend in seamlessly with the philosophy of *samsara* and rebirth.

In each successive birth one can come back as any form of life; a human being in one life can be reborn as one of the lower animals in the next. The plane of existence in which one returns is determined by the Law of Karma. This law states that one's thoughts, words, actions, and deeds in this life have far-reaching ethical consequences, and in fact determine the state of future existence. Those of pure heart and impeccable conduct in this world are guaranteed to be reborn as a higher life form or a high caste person in the next. Those of evil temperament and iniquitous ways are doomed to enter the next world as a dog, an insect, or an outcast. Only by conscientiously performing one's prescribed duties, being true to one's *dharma*, and abstaining from evil thoughts and deeds does a person accumulate enough merit to be assured of a desirable next life. The Law of Karma was neatly stated by rock poet Lou Reed, with his avant-garde band The Velvet Underground, as:

> *Baby, be good*
> *Do what you should*
> *You know it'll be alright.*[17]

Whether this life has been meritorious enough to secure a desirable incarnation next time round remains a great mystery until death, after which good and evil deeds are to be weighed in some cosmic scale of divine retribution, and the next incarnation determined. There is thus a great deal of uncertainty about the form one will take in the world to come, an uncertainty that can only be resolved after death. As Journey sang:

> *Wheel in the sky keeps on turning*
> *I don't know where I'll be tomorrow.*[18]

The picture that seems to emerge is indeed that of a giant cosmic wheel that is constantly revolving, in an endless cycle in which the spark of life is relayed from one birth to the next, to be housed in body after body. The conduct of the current life is the crucial determinant of what follows next in the cycle, so if one has not accomplished sufficient merit by the close of it, a terrible prospect awaits after death. The following lyrics by Eric Clapton's early rock/blues outfit, Cream, neatly sum up the state of affairs:

> *I told you that the light goes up and down*
> *Don't you notice how the wheel goes round?*
> *And you better pick yourself up from the ground*
> *Before they bring the curtain down.*[19]

Many have found in the principles of transmigration and karma an extremely discouraging and pessimistic outlook. An infinity of worldly existences lies stretched out before all people, with no rest in sight. Even if one lives a perfectly blameless and charitable life, the best that can be hoped for is to return to the world as a high-born, but then the agonizing cycle of *samsara* simply begins anew. Lou Reed encapsulated this insufferable situation as:

> *One minute born, one minute doomed*
> *One minute up and one minute down.*[20]

For unfathomable oceans of time, one keeps returning to the worldly plane, having to constantly be on guard lest the slightest misdeed or dark thought cloud the horizon of an unforeseeable future. Such fear of retribution, with the sword of Damocles always hanging over one's head by a thread, would weigh heavy on the strongest of shoulders.

There is, however, a way out from this seemingly ineluctable situation, and that is the way of *moksha*, which means salvation or liberation from the round of rebirths and the miseries of human existence. The attainment of *moksha* is effected by the means already discussed here at length, namely, the extinction of desires and returning to indistinguishable oneness with Brahman. Once this comes about, the highest possible state of existence is reached and one is forever released from the remorseless karmic law. If it is realized that all existence is merely a single energy pulsating in waves, then the crests and troughs of this pulsation can be seen as the processes of birth and death, that is, of *samsara.* Identifying with the energy itself, not its recurring patterns of ebb and flow, is *moksha* — because then you yourself are the eternal energy of the universe and can effortlessly rise above the processes which are the result of its rhythmic fluctuation.

It is worth noting the great dissimilarity between this viewpoint and that of Western religion. In the West, all hope of liberation is pinned on the next world; after death one enters heaven and there enjoys everlasting peace. If one believes in reincarnation, however, the next world promises to be at best a relative improvement on the current situation, and at worst an unimaginable horror. It is more or less a case of "out of the frying pan, into the fire," or, as Lou Reed said:

> *And now I'm set free*
> *I'm set free*
> *I'm set free to find a new illusion.*[21]

Waiting for the afterlife will simply plunge you into *samsara* again, so one had better attain *moksha* now, in this life, for there is no telling when birth as a human will be in the cards again. This is true for the high-born as well as the low-born, for they are both equally caught in the mesh of *Maya* and the spokes of *samsara.* Only by looking beyond the doomed mortal eye and gaining the expansive perspective of the Universal Mind does the fallacy of life, as it is unthinkingly and heedlessly lived, make itself apparent. As Blake said:

> *Some are born to sweet delight*
> *Some are born to endless night*
> *We are led to believe a lie*
> *When we see not thro*[22] *the eye*
> *Which was born in a night, to perish in a night*
> *When the Soul slept in beams of light.*[23]

It is attachment to sense objects and clinging to the ego that keep us in the endless night, chained like Prometheus to the rock of our lower nature, and freedom from them is freedom from the perpetually revolving karmic wheel of endless birth, death, and rebirth.

This truth was discovered by the weather reporter Phil Connors in the movie *Groundhog Day*, when he obtained release from his eternally recurring day only when he renounced his ego-centeredness, gave up his selfish attachment to his needs alone, and worked exclusively for altruistic motives. Since no one else around Connors was aware of the fact that each day was essentially the same one replaying over and over again, he had a special insight into the nature of what was really going on. But as long as he misused this knowledge and employed it for petty personal gain, he was consigned to remain imprisoned in that repetitive and monotonous day. Even attempts at suicide were fruitless, as he still woke up the next morning with the same song playing on the radio, and he would then proceed to meet the same people and undergo the same series of events as every other day. The real change came about when he gave up his narrow focus on his own desires and comforts, and instead put his knowledge to use in helping others and making the world a better place. In the movie, Connors' final release comes when he wins the genuine love of a woman and then he wakes up to a brand new day; this only happens when he surrenders his ego completely. The movie serves as a modern fable illustrating the theories of reincarnation and karma.

Ego Dissolution and The Great Void

The following lines from The Beatles' *Tomorrow Never Knows* are of great significance as they render beautifully in poetic form the core of the mystical experience:

Turn off your mind, relax and float downstream
It is not dying, it is not dying
Lay down all thought, surrender to the void
It is shining, it is shining
That you may see the meaning of within
It is being, it is being.

Given that the forms and images of the world as presented by the senses to our gullible mind are unreal, the only way to experience the reality which is beyond the realm of the senses and conscious thought is to calm and eventually stop the processes and emanations of the mind, which are the origin and cause of the great deception. But this cessation of mind processes leads ultimately to extinction of the ego, to overcoming the identification of the self with "I" and "Me," as distinct from the rest of the universe. This state of being is referred to in Hinduism as *shunyata*, which translates as "nothingness," "the void".

Extinction of the individual consciousness, however, is usually associated with death, for we are accustomed to identifying the self with superficial mental process and the gross, corporeal body, and are simply not attuned to the concept of dissolution of the ego and its absorption into the universe at large while fully awake and conscious.[24] However, it is exactly this state of mind in which primitive cultures exist unconsciously, and it is the conscious attainment of this state that yogis, shamans, and ascetics strive for. Their meditations and selfmortifications are undertaken to achieve this heightened state of existence, to fortify their minds so as not to be terrified when they look within their beings and are confronted with the specter of the swarming universal void which brings forth and consumes all beings and devours all thought. The eternal terror of what awaits after the death of the ego and the material body is expressed by Hamlet, when he contemplates suicide:

> *To die, to sleep;*
> *To sleep, perchance to dream: ay, there's the rub;*
> *For in that sleep of death what dreams may come,*
> *When we have shuffled off this mortal coil,*
> *Must give us pause.*

Hamlet, in this soliloquy, had an intuition of what is written in classic Eastern mystical texts such as the already-mentioned Chinese *The Secret of the Golden Flower* and the Buddhist *The Tibetan Book of the Dead*, both of which state that immediately following the disintegration of consciousness[25] the self will be confronted with horrific images of demons and apparitions, and if they are not recognized as being contents internal to the psyche they will simply seize the mind and rip it to shreds. They are still further illusions that have to be overcome.

The overcoming of the final illusion is said in Buddhism to be the attainment of *nirvana*. *Nirvana* translates as "blown out," "extinguished," where what are extinguished are not only the desires, impulses, hopes and fears of the individual, but the very sense of his separate identity. The clinging of the mind to the idea of itself as an isolated consciousness, existing apart from the world at large, is called *ahankara*[26] in Sanskrit; this has also been translated as "arrogance" and "conceit," reflecting its deluded and utterly flawed mode of conceptualization. The following lines from *The Tibetan Book of the Dead*, where the dead man receives instruction on the true nature of the spirit, impart the same wisdom as the above-quoted lyrics from *Tomorrow Never Knows*, and are in remarkable consonance with them:[27]

> Thine own consciousness, shining, void, and inseparable from the Great Body of Radiance, hath no birth, nor death, and is the Immutable Light — Buddha Amitabha.

In the movement towards enlightenment and *moksha* the ego must be totally discarded in order to let the light from the Great Body of Radiance through, or else the process is not complete. As long as there is an "I" left over that undergoes realization and says "I am enlightened" or "I am one with the Infinite," there exists a duality, however infinitesimal, between the knower and the known. This last vestige of the ego must also be overthrown until there is only Brahman through and through. Once this final overcoming takes place, the blinding radiance of the Great Void bursts through and nothing else can be seen, or remains to be seen.

In his famous self-examination of his thought processes, Descartes came to the conclusion that even if all else is denied — if the senses and consciousness are denounced as mere fabrications of some great unknown deceiver — the very fact of thought, even in the act of being deceived, is proof of the existence of a thinker. In perhaps his most-well known piece of writing Descartes wrote:

> Thus, since our senses sometimes deceive us, I decided to suppose that nothing was exactly as our senses would have us imagine . . . I rejected as false all the reasonings that I had previously taken for

demonstrations. And finally, taking into account the fact that the same thoughts we have when we are awake can also come to us when we are asleep, without any of the latter thoughts being true, I resolved to pretend that everything that had ever entered my mind was no more true than the illusions of my dreams. But immediately afterward I noticed that, during the time I wanted thus to think that everything was false, it was necessary that I, who thought thus, be something. And noticing that this truth — I think, therefore I am — was so firm and so certain that the most extravagant suppositions of the skeptics were unable to shake it, I judged that I could accept it without scruple as the first principle of the philosophy I was seeking.[28]

This is all well in good insofar as it goes, but Descartes, although he did later obvert his proposition and state that if one stops thinking then there is no reason to believe in one's existence, took this to imply that the essence of his substance was to think, that he was a thinking being through and through, and so was entirely distinct from his body. The influence of this Cartesian mind-body cleavage in the development of Western thought was to prove decisive, and continues to be so right through to the present day. Descartes could not conceive of a thought without a thinker, but to the mystics this is the highest order of understanding. They would object strongly to the presence of the "I" that registers the thought process and infers from this that it exists, for it is this very entity that causes the great delusion. Furthermore, to say "I" is to implicitly create a "not-I," and this amounts to demarcating a duality that never existed before. I can only be "me" if there is something I can point to and say that is "not me," thus implying an inherent polarity.

Footnotes

1. Psychoanalytic support is lent to this idea by Freud's use of the term *primal scenes* to denote the earliest experiences of childhood. The word "primal" usually refers to the first age of the world, so here we have a direct correlating in terminology of the earliest phase of life with the earliest phase of the world.
2. This term was coined by Levy-Bruhl to denote the primitive state of non-differentiation between subject and object.
3. Erich Neumann, *The Origins and History of Consciousness.*
4. *Rig Veda*, 10.129.1-2. Translated by Wendy Doniger O'Flaherty.
5. Pink Floyd, *Us and Them.*
6. This freedom from opposites is called *nirdvandva* in Sanskrit.
7. This is said to be the reason that people today wear rings set with precious stones. They are honoring Prometheus for the actions and sufferings he undertook on their behalf.
8. This debasement can be compared to the inability to perceive fully the higher dimensional hyperbody, and the aspect of it that is lost when it manifests itself in the earthly plane.
9. A Jedi knight is an imaginary type of warrior, based on the prototype of a Samurai swordsman or Zen archer.
10. See Illustration 3.
11. The *yin* and the *yang* really represent all pairs of opposites, and are the two archetypal poles of nature. The *yang* is the bright, active, creative, male principle, and the *yin* is the dark, passive, receptive female principle.
12. See Illustration 7.
13. The word Gaia comes from the name of the Greek earth goddess.
14. Bob Dylan, *Subterranean Homesick Blues.*
15. The meaning of this song was famously perverted by the notorious 1960's serial killer Charles Manson, who believed that The Beatles were the four angels of the book of Revelation, and that he was the fifth angel, the resurrected Jesus. He felt that The Beatles were speaking to him directly via their *White Album*, on which the song *Helter Skelter* appears. He interpreted *Helter Skelter* as referring to an impending racial cataclysm in America, in which the black race would rise up and destroy its white oppressors. He even finger-painted the words "Helter Skelter" in blood at the scene of one of his murders. In actuality, Helter Skelter is the British term for a spiral fairground slide.
16. Charles Manson took these lines as a reference to a bottomless pit in the

desert, where The Beatles were telling him and his followers to hide out until the racial war was over and the white race wiped out, after which Manson and the others were to re-emerge and lead the black people.

17. The Velvet Underground, *What Goes On*.

18. Journey, *Wheel in the Sky*.

19. Cream, *Badge*.

20. The Velvet Underground, *What Goes On*.

21. The Velvet Underground, *I'm Set Free*.

22. "Thro'" should be interpreted in the sense of "beyond," not "with".

23. William Blake, *Auguries of Innocence*.

24. This dissolution does occur every night in the state of deep, dreamless sleep, but only after the cognitive functions of the mind have been shut down. Thus, the mystic is actually striving to re-attain the state of mind achieved nightly in sleep, but with his mental faculties alive and receptive to the wondrous energies of this realm.

25. In *The Tibetan Book of the Dead*, this state is called the *Chonyid Bardo*.

26. *Ahankara* corresponds closely to the Greek word *hubris*, meaning arrogant pride or presumption.

27. John Lennon may have had a second-hand acquaintance with these words through his reading of Timothy Leary's *The Psychedelic Experience*, which was a reinterpretation of *The Tibetan Book of the Dead*.

28. Descartes, *Discourse on the Method for Rightly Conducting One's Reason and for Seeking Truth in the Sciences*.

PART TWO

Psychology

CHAPTER 5

MYSTICISM AND PSYCHOLOGY

The Similarities

Psychology and mysticism both regard the realm of consciousness, and of consciously realized thoughts and impulses, as being merely the uppermost layer of the mind, reflecting only the immediate experiences and superficial mental processes of which an individual is aware at any given moment. Furthermore, this upper layer does not present an accurate picture of reality because its contents are subject to a never-ending series of alterations and distortions, to which psychoanalysis gives various names such as sublimation, transference, displacement, etc., and which mysticism refers to as Maya, delusion, avidya.

Both philosophies maintain that beneath the thin, surface-level crust of consciousness lies a vast, in fact infinite, chthonic world of which we are ordinarily unaware, but which contains reality in its undiluted and unaltered form, and which is in a constant dynamic interplay with our everyday hopes, wishes, fears, and fantasies. Psychology calls this world the unconscious, and the mystics call it Brahman, Tao, or any of a host of other names.[1] The two concepts are closely allied.

According to psychoanalytic theory, the mechanism of repression pushes into the unconscious thoughts or feelings that are not compatible with the ideals that either we or society have established, and thereafter it works to ensure that the proscribed material does not resurface into consciousness. The material is certainly real and present, but repression causes us to be blind to its existence, and thus we never really know what is going on within us. The repressed content may eventually show up in consciousness, but only after it has been changed beyond recognition, or had its energies transferred to other areas that are unrelated to the original content.

Like the Eastern sage or master, the psychoanalyst attempts to bring to the surface of mental life the repressed forces and symbols of the unconscious in their *actual*, unmodified form, and to put these liberated unconscious energies to work for the benefit of the individual. Freud wrote:

> We who are analysts set before us as our aim the most complete and profoundest possible analysis of whoever may be our patient. We do not seek to bring him relief by receiving him into the catholic, protestant or socialist community. We seek rather to enrich him from his own internal sources, by putting at the disposal of his ego those energies which, owing to regression, are inaccessibly confined in his unconscious, as well as those which his ego is obliged to squander in the fruitless task of maintaining these repressions.[2]

Or, to put it more compactly, the task of psychoanalysis is to make the unconscious conscious. It is crucial, however, that what is made conscious is experienced *affectively*, with the whole being, rather by the intellect alone. If a patient suffering from a neurosis is informed by the analyst that the root of the problem is a certain traumatic experience in childhood, the patient's mere intellectual registering of this fact (which may be perfectly true) will not magically produce a cure. The experience must be grasped by the whole person, not just the intellect, and then the newly-uncovered unconscious content needs to be reintegrated into consciousness. As long as the patient is simply told about the fact, and as long as he continues to observe it from a distance as if it were an object removed from him, no healing transformation is possible.

The analysis of the problem and discovery of the cause are certainly the first steps on the road to recovery, but only when the patient intuitively, affectively, and wholly *experiences* the unconscious fact and becomes awake and alive to its presence, only then is a cure effected in any meaningful way. It is as if someone is simply told that a throbbing pain in his/her hand is caused by a splinter that is lodged in the palm, and then nothing further is done about it. While there is no doubt about the accuracy of the statement, relief from the pain can only come about when the splinter is confronted and removed. As Erich Fromm explains it:

> As long as the patient remains in the attitude of a detached scientific observer, taking himself as the object of his investigation, he is not in touch with his unconscious, except by thinking about it; he does not experience the wider, deeper reality within himself. Discovering one's unconscious is, precisely, not an intellectual act, but an affective experience, which can hardly be put into words, if at all . . . The process of discovering the unconscious can be described as a series of ever-widening experiences, which are felt deeply and which transcend theoretical, intellectual knowledge.[3]

When interpreted in this light, the song *I Can See Clearly Now*, written by Johnny Nash, is in concurrence with the idea that once the obstructions in the path to the unconscious source of pain are removed then the malaise is lifted and the spirit unburdened. The lyrics to this song are reproduced in full below:

> *I can see clearly now, the rain has gone*
> *I can see all obstacles in my way*
> *Gone are the dark clouds that had me blind*
> *It's gonna be a bright, bright sunshiny day*
> *It's gonna be a bright, bright sunshiny day*
>
> *I think I can make it now, the pain has gone*
> *All of the bad feelings have disappeared*
> *Here is the rainbow I've been praying for*
> *It's gonna be a bright, bright sunshiny day*
> *It's gonna be a bright, bright sunshiny day*
>
> *Look all around there's nothing but blue sky*
> *Look straight ahead, there's nothing but blue sky!*

Different psychological systems often disagree among themselves as to the exact nature and contents of the unconscious, and about the methods needed to remove these dark clouds and obstacles. But whether these contents are said to be the repressed sexual traumas and incest wishes of early childhood, as Freud claimed, or Jung's archetypes of the collective unconscious,[4] or Adler's will to power, or any of a host of other complexes, drives, and motivations that have been variously proposed, there is near universal agreement that these contents are unconscious, and that they need to be realized and experienced by consciousness if human development is to take place. Mysticism goes even further, in fact all the way, and says that the whole of the unconscious, each and every facet of life and the world that is hidden from us, must be brought to the surface, thus leading to an infinite explosion of limited consciousness into cosmic consciousness until only the Universal Self remains. The concluding lines of *I Can See Clearly Now* hint at such an intimation of all-containing oneness.

The Differences

Despite their many similarities and points of contact, it must be recognized that Western psychology and Eastern mysticism are not identical, and that there exist some very fundamental differences between them. Psychology generally limits its concern to the individual mind, for nothing beyond it can be definitively known or asserted, and since psychology has its roots in the Western scientific tradition it requires proofs for all assertions and claims. Thus, it treats the mind as an isolated sphere, disconnected from its primordial oneness with the universe.

Mysticism, in contrast, seeks to restore the severed link between individual mind and Universal Mind. It contends that what is hidden from us by *Maya* are not just mental processes and impulses, but the very nature of the external world, our society, and the total experience of the total being. Freud provided an important clue to an understanding and synthesis of both concepts when he wrote:

In psychoanalysis there is no choice for us but to assert that mental processes are in themselves unconscious, and to liken the perception of them by means of consciousness to the perception of the external world by means of the sense-organs . . . Like the physical, the psychical is not necessarily in reality what it appears to us to be.[5]

This comparison weaves the threads of psychoanalysis and mysticism into a single fabric and unifies their fields of interest into one all-encompassing realm: the hidden world of the unconscious. However, while both systems aim at a transformation of consciousness, they differ markedly in the nature and purpose of this transformation. The goal of the psychoanalyst is to return to health and normalcy a person suffering from a mental disorder, whereas the mystic aims at going beyond such states of "normalcy" by extinguishing his very identity as an isolated ego and merging it with the supra-consciousness of which his and all other egos are but individual, ephemeral manifestations. The psychotherapist aims at transforming the consciousness of sick or disturbed people, whereas Buddhism, Taoism, and Hinduism aim at transforming the consciousness of perfectly normal, socially adjusted people such that they recognize the misapprehension which they and all others thus far have been laboring under. As Joseph Campbell says:

> Psychoanalysis is a technique to cure excessively suffering individuals of the unconsciously misdirected desires and hostilities that weave around them their private webs of unreal terrors and ambivalent attractions; the patient released from these finds himself able to participate with comparative satisfaction in the more realistic fears, hostilities, erotic and religious practices, business enterprises, wars, pastimes, and household tasks offered to him by his particular culture. But for the one who has deliberately undertaken the difficult and dangerous journey beyond the village compound,[6] these interests, too, are to be regarded as based on error. Therefore the aim of religious teaching is not to cure the individual back again to the general delusion, but to detach him from delusion altogether; and this is not by readjusting the desire (eros) and hostility (thanatos) — for that would only originate a new context of delusion — but by extinguishing the impulses to the very root .[7]

Contemporary musicians have also delved into the mystery of the unknown self within, and have often described the nature of the universe and the functions of the unconscious in words and images that are perfectly compatible with the observations of psychologists and mystics. Indeed, the artist is better able to describe the glimpse he has been afforded of the enduring mystery of life because he has the power of creative expression at his command, as well as a greater wealth of abstract and symbolic representation from which to draw; such representation is the closest we can hope to get to a description of enlightenment without having experienced it for ourselves. The artist is naturally endowed with the gifts necessary to make the unconscious conscious.

The Nature of the Unconscious

As discussed previously, the nature of the unconscious, the original state of the mind of man, is one in which all opposites and seemingly contradictory elements are united and intermingled. To the mind of modern, civilized humanity, far removed from its unconscious moorings, the union of opposites and the blending together of seemingly antithetical concepts results in bewildering paradoxes and conundrums, but to the primitive and the yogi it is a completely natural experience, and is in fact perfectly in tune with inner realities. It is precisely this original, forgotten state that the mystic aspires to re-attain, and for this he must quiet the workings of the ego and the empirical mind, which are later products of evolution.

It is also within these primordial depths of the individual that the modern psychoanalyst looks for the source and resolution of the mental and psychical disturbances which afflict so many people today; for the unconscious is the source both of universal revelation and of mental disorders, and whether one or the other of these states of mind exerts its influence over an individual depends on his/her level of control and mastery of the will.

The classic analogy is that of a charioteer who has to tame the powerful, yet extremely wild and capricious, horses that are pulling his chariot, and to make them submit to his command. If he is successful, he has at his disposal awesome power to achieve his difficult goal. If not, he is dragged unwilling wherever the horses choose to take him and is left at their mercy.[8]

The mystics and the psychologists both regard the unconscious or One Mind as being beyond the spatio-temporal world, and as being the source of all forms and images. The *collective unconscious* in Jung's analytical psychology is precisely such a substratum common to the psyche of all human beings and in which all images and categories of thought have their origin. Even Freud, who has often been criticized for interpreting symbolic and transpersonal psychological factors too literally and with an excessively personalistic bias, spoke of the unconscious as timeless, as a place where opposing and antithetical influences, motives and intentions are to be found juxtaposed. In the following extract from his writings he discusses the characteristics of the two systems: consciousness (Cs.) and unconscious (Ucs.):

> The nucleus of the Ucs. consists of . . . wishful impulses. These instinctual impulses are co-ordinated with one another, exist side by side without being influenced by one another, and are exempt from mutual contradiction. When two wishful impulses whose aims must appear to us incompatible become simultaneously active, the two impulses do not diminish each other or cancel each other out, but combine to form an intermediate aim, a compromise.

> . . . The processes of the system Ucs. are timeless; i.e. they are not ordered temporally, are not altered by the passage of time; they have no reference to time at all. Reference to time is bound up, once again, with the work of the system Cs.[9]

The person who discovers the unconscious, concealed realm within himself (either creatively, through spiritual mastery, or destructively, through a breakdown of mental functioning), with all its complexities, subtleties and infinite power, is initially disoriented and bewildered by the seeming chaos swirling within the depths, where all dualities and opposites blend into one pure substance. Bob Dylan describes the overwhelming confusion that is encountered there:

> *Now everything's a little upside down*
> *As a matter of fact the wheels have stopped*
> *What's good is bad, what's bad is good*

You'll find out when you reach the top
You're on the bottom.[10]

Imbalance and Compensation

In the Chinese symbol of the *yin-yang,* polar opposites support and sustain each other in a delicate balance. If there is an excess or preponderance of one, the other correspondingly increases in strength, although in subtle and insidious ways. When the light of the *yang* reaches its highest intensity, the darkness of the *yin* is at its blackest. The nature of the unconscious in its totality is that of the *yin-yang* union, and any attempt by consciousness to engender a violent split between the two can only lead to catastrophic consequences, for the intrinsic harmony of nature will have been violated.

Carl Jung took the concept of the unification of diametrically opposed factors within the unconscious and encapsulated it in his theory of *enantiodromia,* which translates as "running to the opposite." According to this theory, a balance needs to be maintained in consciousness between both of a pair of opposing psychic tendencies. If the conscious attitude lays too great an emphasis on one half of the pair, the imbalance is compensated by an exaggeration and strengthening within the unconscious of the half which consciousness has stifled or repressed. This leads to an irrational and infantile complex within the unconscious that behaves in direct contrast to the tendency that has been exclusively selected by consciousness, and leads to a split within the individual's personality.

To illustrate this point Jung, in his book *Psychological Types,* gives the example of a person who struggled for years in the printing trade until he eventually became the owner of a flourishing business. This business expanded to such an extent that it consumed all his energies, and left him no time for anything else whatsoever. To compensate for this conscious over-emphasis on material pursuits, his unconscious reactivated his childhood interest in painting and drawing, with disastrous results. He tried to incorporate his newfound artistic sensibilities into his products, but the result was so infantile and inappropriate that his business collapsed. The irrational attitude that formed in his unconscious, as a direct counterbalancing force to the attitude that received excessive conscious focus, led to his downfall.

A classical example of the same process can be drawn from the Biblical tale of Nebuchadnezzar, as recounted in the Book of Daniel. Nebuchadnezzar was the mighty King of Babylon (reigned 605 — 562 B.C.), and one of the most powerful rulers of his day. His conquests were many,[11] and under him Babylon became the most magnificent city in the world.[12] He became so conceited because of his might and accomplishments that he had a ninety-feet high golden statue of himself built, and ordered that all people worship him as God.

However, one night he had a dream in which his downfall was foretold. In time, the prophecy came true, and Nebuchadnezzar was cast out from the world of men and condemned to live like an animal. His hair and nails grew untrimmed, and he ate grass "in the manner of oxen." After seven years in the wilderness his understanding returned, and he then offered praise to the one true God, the higher power that lives forever and whose dominion is everlasting.

Nebuchadnezzar's one-sided exaggeration and pride in his conscious achievements resulted in a massive psychic inflation of his ego, to the extent that he believed himself to be almighty God. The unconscious, however, balked at this appalling disproportion, and caused a reaction just as extreme in the opposite direction to thwart the monstrous elevation of the ego, reducing Nebuchadnezzar from a conquering hero to a pitiful, subhuman creature.

Bob Dylan, in the lyrics below, has also provided an enduring image of a fallen titan, a once-mighty hero who is now dethroned and degraded because of his inflated pride, his bloated *ahankara*:

Once upon a time you dressed so fine
Threw the bums a dime, in your prime
Didn't you
People called, said "Beware doll,
You're bound to fall"
You thought they were all
Kiddin' you
You used to laugh about
Everybody that was hangin' out
Now you don't talk so loud

Now you don't seem so proud
About having to be scrounging around
For your next meal.

How does it feel?
How does it feel?
To be without a home
Like a complete unknown
Like a rolling stone...[13]

Like Jung, Freud also stated that any repressed unconscious tendency can find conscious expression in its exact opposite after passing through the filtering and distorting process (*reaction formation*) that it must undergo before entering the conscious arena. In many of his case studies he found that profuse expressions of love towards a person often masked underlying antipathy and resentment, and vice versa.[14] In short, there is a constant and dynamic interplay in the unconscious between all opposites, and they are not to be seen as fundamentally disparate forces. All students of the mind and seekers of the self, throughout the ages, have been in agreement about the truth of this fundamental and indisputable fact.

Footnotes

1. Names are of no significance, for they are simply different labels for the one underlying unity. For, as we read in Shakespeare's *Romeo and Juliet*, "What's in a name? That which we call a rose, by any other name would smell as sweet."

2. S. Freud, *The Question of Lay Analysis*.

3. Erich Fromm, D. T. Suzuki, and Richard de Martino, *Zen Buddhism and Psychoanalysis*.

4. These are discussed at length in the following chapter.

5. S. Freud, *The Unconscious*.

6. Ie., the mystic. Campbell's portrayal of the mystic as a heroic adventurer who journeys beyond his familiar, everyday world is dealt with further in Part 3.

7. Joseph Campbell, *The Hero with a Thousand Faces*.

8. This analogy has been used in many cultures and many contexts. For example:

   a) Plato has likened the soul to a winged charioteer driving a pair of horses. One of the horses is of good stock and obeys the master's command, while the other is precisely the opposite, being possessed of a vicious and unyielding nature. It is the function of the charioteer to drive the chariot up into the highest heavens, where the soul can experience for itself the glorious sights of the divine region, but he is hindered in his task because the bad horse refuses to cooperate. The degree to which the soul can experience the divine depends on the extent to which the recalcitrant horse can be controlled. The more the charioteer can bend the horse to his will and make his team act in unison, the more like a god he becomes. In *Phaedrus* Plato says:

      > The teams of the gods, which are well matched and tractable, go easily, but the rest with difficulty; for the horse with the vicious nature, if he has not been well broken in, drags his driver down by throwing all his weight in the direction of the earth; supreme then is the agony of the struggle which awaits the soul.

   b) Freud drew on a similar analogy when describing the relation of the ego to the id, where the id is the deep layer of powerful primitive urges within man that obeys the pleasure principle, and the ego is the rational function of the mind that obeys the reality principle, which must temper the aggressive demands of the id by taking into account practical considerations and deciding the most reasonable and appropriate course of action to be taken in a particular situation. In *The Ego and the Id*, Freud writes:

> The functional importance of the ego is manifested in the fact that normally control over the approaches to motility devolves upon it. Thus in its relations to the id it is like a man on horseback, who has to hold in check the superior strength of the horse.

c) The Katha Upanishad also, like Plato, uses the analogy of the soul (Atman) as the owner of a chariot, and, like Freud, assigns the task of the charioteer to reason (ego). It says:

> Know the Atman as the Lord of a chariot; and the body as the chariot itself. Know that reason is the charioteer; and the mind indeed is the rein.
>
> The horses, they say, are the senses; and their paths are the objects of sense...
>
> He who has not right understanding and whose mind is never steady is not the ruler of his life, like a bad driver with wild horses.
>
> But he who has right understanding, and whose mind is ever steady is the ruler of his life, like a good driver with well-trained horses.
>
> ... The man whose chariot is driven by reason, who watches and holds the reins of his mind, reaches the End of the journey, the supreme everlasting Spirit.

d) With these analogies and descriptions in mind, it is worth noting the following lines from The Rolling Stones' *Wild Horses*:

> *Wild horses couldn't drag me away*
> *Wild, wild horses*
> *We'll ride them some day.*

9. S. Freud, *The Unconscious.*
10. Bob Dylan, *Idiot Wind.*
11. Including that of Jerusalem, upon the sack of which he took the Jews to Babylon to remain there in captivity.
12. The hanging gardens of Babylon built by him are still considered to have been one the Seven Wonders of the World.
13. Bob Dylan, *Like a Rolling Stone.*
14. One of the better-known examples of reaction-formation is that of Freud's description of the anal character, whose overemphasis on cleanliness and orderliness is a reaction-formation against the uncleanliness and repellant messiness of the anal zone, to which he is fixated.

CHAPTER 6

MIND, WORLD AND PROJECTION

The Mind and Its Productions

We have seen that both the mystics and the psychologists claim that we simply cannot put any faith in the picture of the world as it is presented to us by our mental images, which in turn are derived from the sensory organs and instincts. How is one to ascertain the reality of an object that one touches or sees?

When a sense organ receives a stimulus or excitation it relays this information by sending electrical signals that travel along the nerve cells to the brain, which then makes the impression known to consciousness. But there are many points in this series of events which are based entirely on the specific, subjective conditions of the perceiving individual, and hence the end product of the series, the conscious impression, cannot be presumed to have any objective validity whatsoever. In the case of sensory stimulation, people have varying thresholds of sensitivity to stimuli, and so different people will register the same external fact differently. In instances of paralysis or sensory dysfunction (such as blindness), the stimulus does not even cross the threshold. So, an external fact is only felt to be real and present to the extent that it is acknowledged by the mind. Even when an object or thought does make its way through to the sphere of cognition, the subjective factor matches it to some existing psychic pattern and modifies it accordingly, and so again the mind plays a crucial role in molding and shaping the nature of cognition and perception. One is drawn again and again to the inescapable conclusion that the mind alone is the sole arbiter of all images, categories, and distinctions in the world, that all of these are different in the case of each individual, and that they are dependent on his or her sensory apparatus and mental faculties.

These observations are also confirmed by neuroscience. From a purely neurophysiological point of view, sensations and motor activity arise from various specialized centers within the cerebral cortex of the brain. Very roughly speaking, different centers within the cortex are connected to nerve endings in the body by a chain of intervening nerve cells and the synapses, or junctions, between them. When a nerve ending is stimulated, the associated cortical center receives electrical impulses that travel to it along the synapses, and then it triggers the "appropriate" sensation based upon subjective interpretation. The reason that the word "appropriate" appears in quotation marks is that the sensation which is experienced as a result of cerebral activity is in fact completely arbitrary, and is subject to conditioning. To use a crude analogy, the nerves provide the building blocks to the mind, and what the mind decides to construct with those blocks is up to it.

For example, the eye sees an object when photon packets arriving from the object strike the retinal surface, and thus stimulate it.[1] This stimulation is then relayed to the brain via the optic nerve, and the result is a visual impression of the object. What is interesting is that the image of the object as it appears on the retina is actually inverted, or upside-down, and the mind automatically flips the image so that it looks the right way up to us.

What all this goes to show is that there are two processes taking place here: the excitation of a nerve ending, and the subjective interpretation of that excitation by the mind which results in a certain impression being produced. Thus, we do not experience raw currents of electrical energy or photon packets, but instead "feel" the sand running through our fingers and "see" the colors of the rainbow. These impressions could easily be felt as something totally different, but our nature has conditioned us to see and feel in one way and not another. In fact, there is no way of knowing that what I call "seeing" is not what another person experiences as (what I call) "hearing." We could all simply have learned to call different types of sense impressions by the same names, even though our subjective experiences of them are completely different.

As an example, consider the different perspectives of an average person and a highly discerning Chinese sage. When the average person looks at an object he sees a firm, well-defined entity, delimited in space by its boundary. The Chinese sage, on the other hand, sees the object merely as a temporary crystallization of dynamic energy, interacting freely with its environment. Everything is based on the relative viewpoint of the perceiver.

This fact is nicely demonstrated by the parable of the blind men and the elephant, which has long been used in the East to show the personally-conditioned nature of all sense perception, and was rendered in poetic form by John Godfrey Saxe in the nineteenth century.[2] In Saxe's version, six blind men are led to an elephant and asked to describe it. The blind men in turn feel the side, tusk, trunk, knee, ear, and tail of the elephant and they assert, respectively, that the creature is like a wall, a spear, a snake, a tree, a fan, and a rope. What they all *called* "elephant" was in fact a completely different *inner experience* for each of them.

It is interesting to note that when a change in the state of consciousness occurs, such as in a mystical or psychedelically-induced experience, the rigid patterns of neurological functioning are often loosened, and the lines dividing various impressions arising from aural or visual cues are blurred. The world seems to become more fluid and dynamic, and sensory impressions often melt and intermingle with each other. In this state of altered consciousness (technically known as *synesthesia*) people often talk of seeing a mosaic of colors or visual images when listening to a piece of music, and other such instances of perceptual commingling. In precisely such a condition of psychedelically altered perception (via LSD), Alan Watts wrote the following lines about his new perspective on the world:

> Thus transformed into consciousness, into the electric, interior luminosity of the nerves, the world seems vaguely insubstantial — devel-

oped upon a color film, resounding upon the skin of a drum, pressing, not with weight, but with vibrations interpreted as weight. Solidity is a neurological invention. . .

The physical world is vibration, quanta, but vibrations of what? To the eye, form and color; to the ear, sound; to the nose, scent; to the fingers, touch. But these are all different languages for the same thing, different qualities of sensitivity, different dimensions of conscious-ness. The question, "Of what are they differing forms?" seems to have no meaning. What is light to the eye is sound to the ear. I have the image of the senses being terms, forms, or dimensions not of one thing common to all, but of each other, locked in a circle of mutuality. Closely examined, shape becomes color, which becomes vibration, which becomes sound, which becomes smell, which becomes taste, and then touch, and then again shape. . . I see all these sensory dimen-sions as a round dance, gesticulations of one pattern being trans-formed into gesticulations of another.[3]

Another example of this type of blending together of sensory im-pressions is provided in the following lines by Bob Dylan:

Far between sundown's finish and midnight's broken toll
We ducked inside the doorway, thunder crashing
As majestic bells of bolts struck shadows in the sounds
Seeming to be the chimes of freedom flashing.[4]

So, it is only the fixed grooves of inherited and learned patterns of perceptual and sensory interpretation that determine how we view the world, and our place in it. If the technology were sophisticated enough, and somebody were to attach electrodes or computer chips to the brain and send electrical signals directly to certain neural centers, they could in theory create an alternative universe for us, complete with memories and reminiscences, that would be every bit as real and convincing as the one we live in now. This theme has been explored variously in mov-ies such as *Blade Runner*, *Total Recall*, and *The Matrix*.

Even discounting such purely theoretical and fanciful ideas, it is an undeniable fact that cerebral centers do sometimes trigger sensations spontaneously, without any external excitation, such as when people feel hysterical (or phantom) pain in an amputated limb or when they see mirages. Given that this is so, how is it possible to dismiss the doubt that all cerebral excitations are merely hysterical productions or the result of spontaneous eruptions of neural electrical energy? It is, plainly, not possible to discount this possibility, and so the nature of all we have been taught and which we hold so dear, must be regarded as based on the flimsiest of premises. It is simply to be regarded as the best that we could do given that our physical limitations prevent us from comprehending anything more profound. When, or rather if, we progress further in our understanding of the labyrinth of the mind, our modes of perception and cognition will change and evolve accordingly to reflect the fact that subjective and objective reality are in actuality one and the same thing.

Therefore, the only logical conclusion that can be drawn from all of these considerations is that the notion of an external world "out there," filled with solid blocks of matter which are perceived by billions of isolated, short-lived bubbles of body-enclosed consciousness, is untenable because there is simply no justification for it. There are only mental states, and our experience of the world is simply what we have been conditioned to interpret these mental states as meaning and signifying.

Before delving into the contemporary psychological theories (and the related insights by musicians) concerning the mental structures and functions pertaining to the projecting of the images of the world as we see it, it is edifying to first examine briefly the work of Descartes in that area, which of course preceded the modern psychologists and presaged some of their work. His treatment of the subject was wonderfully lucid, insightful, and untainted by prejudice. He set out to examine the process by which we gain knowledge or ideas about the external world, and did his utmost to ensure that his conclusions were not influenced by things he had learned or taken for granted. The first thing to consider was the argument that, since the feeling or idea of an object usually comes to a person independently of his will, and often against it, it must be the case that the object is external to him and is sending its likeness to him. Descartes wrote:

> I must inquire particularly into those ideas that I believe to be derived from things existing outside me. Just what reason do I have for believ-

ing that these ideas resemble those things? Well, I do seem to have been taught so by nature. Moreover, I do know from experience that these ideas do not depend upon my will, nor consequently upon myself, for I often notice them even against my will. Now, for example, whether or not I will it, I feel heat. It is for this reason that I believe this feeling or idea of heat comes to me from something other than myself, namely from the heat of the fire by which I am sitting. Nothing is more obvious than the judgment that this thing is sending its likeness rather than something else into me.[5]

Descartes realized at this point the folly of basing his argument on having been "taught so by nature," which amounted to putting undue faith in fickle impulses and drives (which had often caused him to make poor judgments in the past). So, he continued his discourse by rejecting that which seemed "obvious" or "natural" as being an unreliable indicator of the true nature of things, for there is no way to ascertain what "obvious" or "natural" really means. He then went on to write:

Although these ideas do not depend upon my will, it does not follow that they necessarily proceed from things existing outside me. For just as these impulses about which I spoke just now seem to be different from my will, even though they are in me, so too perhaps there is also in me some other faculty, one not yet sufficiently known to me, which produces these ideas, just as it has always seemed up to now that ideas are formed in me without any help from external things when I am asleep.

Thus, proceeding from a rational analysis of the world and the self, we now arrive in Western philosophy at the idea of an internal mechanism projecting or creating illusory ideas, a mechanism that was proposed more than a millennium earlier by the great minds of the East as *Maya*. With this introductory discussion of the classical view on the subject, we can now turn to the modern approach to it.

Archetypes and the Collective Unconscious

In the song *Mind Games*, John Lennon achieves a wonderful synthesis between elements of the mystical, philosophical, and psychological observations discussed thus far. His words below, from that song, find resonance both in ancient wisdom and in modern psychology:

We're playing those mind games forever
Projecting our images in space and in time.

This elaborates further on the role of the subjective factor in apperception, and on the nature of *Maya*. *Maya* is the internal source that projects the illusory image of our self and the world, and leads us to believe that it is real. It is contained within us, and projects outward. Our true nature, and that of all things, is infinite and eternal, yet the psyche projects its images onto the exterior world as discontinuous forms and then regards them as discrete entities bounded by space and limited by time. The idea of projection as a fundamental psychological function of the unconscious mind has also been postulated by Freud and Jung. This function plays an extremely important role in Jungian psychology, and therefore it is worthwhile to discuss it at further length.

In Jung's theory, that portion of an individual's unconscious mind which is unique to him and is shaped according to his particular experiences and influences is termed the *personal unconscious*. This is more or less the unconscious layer that is dealt with in Freudian psychoanalysis, with all its emphasis on infantile sexuality and childhood sexual researches in determining the course that a person's mental development takes.

According to Jung, however, in addition to consciousness and the personal unconscious, which are different and unique to every individual, the human mind has a deeper unconscious sub-stratum that has existed since the dawn of mankind, and which all human beings have in common. This layer he called the *collective unconscious*, which contains primordial images that have been imprinted upon it by the various evolving forms of life that have existed upon the earth. He termed these images the *archetypes*[6] of the collective unconscious, and these archetypes exist in all people as organs of the psyche. Just as all people have a common physical structure which consists of a head, arms, legs, etc., so they have a common psychical structure which is composed of the archetypes. They are deposits of human experience stretching back to its earliest beginnings, still extant within the furthermost recesses of the mind, and shared by humanity at large (as well as by animals).

These archetypes exist deep in the collective unconscious; they are to be found in humans at all times and in all places, and they project their images upon the conscious mind (which is a relatively late development in the history of humanity). And because the archetypes are everywhere and in all conditions the same, the images projected by them are also everywhere the same, although with slight modifications according to local and historical circumstances. Hence the fact that all myths have common universal motifs, although these are clothed in the garb of each particular culture.

The personal unconscious, then, can be seen to be the deposit of empirical experience acquired directly in a person's lifetime. The archetypes of the collective unconscious, on the other hand, exist *a priori* and are antecedent to the personal history of the individual. They are present in all people from the moment of birth, and even before.

A few extracts from Jung's own writings will help clarify these concepts further. Of the personal unconscious, he writes:

> The materials contained in this layer are of a personal nature in so far as they have the character partly of acquisitions derived from the individual's life and partly of psychological factors which could just as well be conscious. . . We recognize them as personal contents because their effects, or their partial manifestation, or their source can be discovered in our personal past.[7]

And of the collective unconscious, he writes:

> In addition to our immediate consciousness, which is of a thoroughly personal nature and which we believe to be the only empirical psyche (even if we tack on the personal unconscious as an appendix), there exists a second psychic system of a collective, universal, and impersonal nature which is identical in all individuals. This collective un-

conscious does not develop individually but is inherited. It consists of pre-existent forms, the archetypes, which can only become conscious secondarily and which give definite form to certain psychic contents.[8]

Thus, mythological motifs such as the Virgin Birth and the Hero Journey, and categorical constructions of the mind such as Time and Space, are also projections of the archetypes, which, as Jung says, can only become conscious secondarily, i.e. via projection upon the plane of conscious thought. In the primal region of the collective unconscious, which is independent of categories such as space and time, and where all polar opposites exist as a hermetic unity, psychic contents are undifferentiated, but in the course of history they have become constellated into archetypes, and when they are projected onto the waking mind they appear as distinct entities and images.

In this manner, an archetypal intuition of the all-pervading, unmanifest One Soul is projected onto consciousness as a personalistic father-deity or God image. The ultimate archetype of Brahman or Tao is forever and always the same, but the projections of it are multifarious — Yahweh, Christ, Krishna, Church, State; similarly, the archetype of the Eternal Feminine (or anima, in Jung's terminology) is projected onto an actual person that a given individual knows or meets, and to whom a mysterious allure thus attaches itself. These symbolic projections are the only means we have of understanding to even the slightest extent the contents of so complex a structure as the psyche. Jung says:

> The psyche is something so highly complicated, so vast in extent, and so rich in elements unknown to us, and its aspects overlap and interweave with one another in such an amazing degree, that we always turn to symbols in order to try to represent what we know about it.[9]

Therefore, the external world in which we live our everyday lives, and our inner self which we ordinarily identify with the physical body, are indeed, as Lennon says, mind games that we have been playing forever, or at least since the modern conscious mind split off from its primordial, unconscious root. The action of *Maya* causes us to mistake the manifold projections of our mind for reality, and to remain ignorant of the fact that the source of these projections is common to all of us.

Even Freud, from whose ranks Jung broke because of the former's excessive focus and almost occult belief in the role of sexuality and infantile sexual experiences in the formation of neuroses, acknowledged the existence of a collective mind and the transmission of psychical data down through the generations. He wrote:

> Without the assumption of a collective mind, which makes it possible to neglect the interruptions of mental acts caused by the extinction of the individual, social psychology in general cannot exist. Unless psychical processes were continued from one generation to another, if each generation were obliged to acquire its attitude to life anew, there would be no progress in this field, and next to no development. . . Social psychology shows very little interest, on the whole, in the manner in which the required continuity in the mental life of successive generations is established. A part of the problem seems to be met by the inheritance of psychical dispositions which, however, need to be given some sort of impetus in the life of the individual before they can be roused into actual operation.[10]

Of course, Freud did not proceed with this line of thinking further, whereas Jung made it the cornerstone of his psychological theory.[11] Also, Freud saw mental dispositions as being passed on from one generation of human beings to the next, whereas Jung claimed that the collective unconscious predates human existence and, at its deepest strata, is even shared with the lowest life forms. He wrote:

> In its development and structure, it still preserves elements that connect it with the invertebrates and ultimately with the protozoa. Theoretically it should be possible to "peel" the collective unconscious, layer by layer, until we came to the psychology of the worm, and even of the amoeba.[12]

This explains the kinship many primitive people and cultures feel with animals and plants, which are often elevated to the status of totem ancestors and sacramental offerings, for these people recognize that at the most fundamental level all life is the same. This is also why Buddhism and ascetic religions like Jainism[13] insist that each and every living, sentient creature is precious and that its life should be preserved at all costs. This is the philosophy of *ahimsa*, non-violence or non-injury, and this idea was recently brought to widespread awareness due to its adoption by Mahatma Gandhi, who was influenced by Jainism in his early life. In the most orthodox form of Jainism, the lives of insects and even bacteria are considered sacred and so Jain monks carry a broom to sweep the path before them lest they inadvertently trample on any creature, and they cover their mouths with a piece of cloth so that tiny organisms may not be carried into them.

So, the archetypes, as defined by Jung, represent that which is eternal in man, stretching back to the earliest beginnings of life itself, and they continue to live on in every single person, making themselves known to consciousness via symbols and projections which correspond directly to the images of dream and myth. Thus, dreams and myths represent in symbolic or pictorial form a hidden component of the unconscious, and by following the path pointed to by the symbol we arrive directly at the archetype, an achievement of shattering impact.

In the beginning of the movie *2001: A Space Odyssey*, which depicts the dawn of human history, a mysterious monolith appears before the pre-human ape-creatures that are roaming the earth, and it appears again towards the end of the movie when eons have passed and man has made the ultimate technological advancement of creating intelligent computers and machines capable of penetrating into deep space. This monolith symbolizes the existence of the archetypes of the collective unconscious. As archetypes existed in the pre-human mists of the past, so the monolith is present before the first ape-like humans in the movie, and as the archetypes are passed on through the ages from generation to generation, so the monolith is also present in the far-flung future.

Furthermore, this monolith serves as a portal to the untapped and unutilized energies of the mind. When the astronaut, David Bowman, passes through the monolith, he watches transfixed as a cosmic symphony of visions unfolds before his eyes and the universe reveals itself to him in its uninhibited glory.[14] Having unlocked the archetype and set free the caged powers of his mind, he has reached the plane of existence spoken of by the saints and mystics as liberation — the realization of his universal self. This is a profound spiritual rebirth, and in the movie Bowman is reborn as a Star Baby, a new celestial body, luminous, cosmic, and universal.

The archetypes of the collective unconscious can thus be seen to be charged with primitive psychic energy, or *mana*, and to experience them directly via ritual, art, or myth, as opposed to secondarily via projections, is to open up a similar portal to cosmic energies within us of unimaginable intensity.

Childhood Psyche

In Jungian psychology, the collective unconscious is considered a timeless repository of the psychic content of all of humanity. Thus, when a child is born it carries within it the history of its race, the images and archetypes that have been passed on to it from its earliest ancestors. It is originally in the same state of complete submergence in the unconscious as were the first humans, and over the course of its life the child re-lives all the stages of conscious evolutionary development through which the human race as a whole has progressed. Seen in this light, the following lyrics from Bob Dylan's *Lord Protect My Child* seem in complete agreement with Jung's theory of the transmission of primordial psychic data from time immemorial:

> As his youth now unfolds
> He is centuries old.

Compare this with the following passage from Erich Neumann on the psychology of the child:

> In the child the great images and archetypes of the collective unconscious are living reality, and very close to him; indeed, many of his sayings and reactions, questions and answers, dreams and images, express this knowledge which still derives from his prenatal existence. It is transpersonal experience not personally acquired, a possession acquired from "over there." Such knowledge is rightly regarded as ancestral knowledge, and the child as a reborn forebear.[15]

Therefore each of us, when we were children, originally experienced firsthand a vision of Paradise before it was corrupted by the knowledge of opposites that is acquired as we grow and as the ego forms and develops, until finally the glorious vision is completely shut out by the screen of consciousness. This is the vision that the mystic and sage are trying to rediscover by halting the processes of the rational mind that began when childhood ended. Hence, the saying of Jesus: "Except ye be converted, and become as little children, ye shall not enter into the kingdom of heaven."[16] Thus also the Taoist sage's high praise for the infant, childlike state. The Tao Te Ching says:

> *Can you keep the spirit and embrace the One without departing from them?*
> *Can you concentrate your vital force and achieve the highest degree of weakness like an infant?*

The infant is thus seen to be close to the Universal Spirit; it has only recently been parted from it and so still has shining, vivid memories of it. The Pink Floyd song, *Shine On, You Crazy Diamond*, begins with the words:

> *Remember when you were young*
> *You shone like the sun.*

This clearly identifies the state of childhood with solar consciousness.[17] When we were born, our consciousness was that of the eternal sun, but since then it has been eclipsed and blotted out by the temporal moon. Given the profoundly mystical nature of childhood, it is hardly to be wondered at that every person longs for a return to those halcyon days, which are remembered with a rosy glow of nostalgia as being magical and enchanted; for a return to childhood is a return to the perfect, blissful state of containment in the mother's womb, of self-dissolution and total immersion in the unconscious.

In the movie *Citizen Kane*, Kane's dying word is "Rosebud," the name of a snow-sled he played with in childhood. Even after scaling the heights of wealth and power, in life, he died lonely and friendless, and in his final moments he clung to the memory of the days when all around was experienced as bliss, perfection, and contentment.

We have to re-discover the dream of Paradise we briefly glimpsed in childhood, before we were cast out for tasting the forbidden fruit of knowledge. The world must be seen once again as it is, free from the projections of the image-creating mind and from the productions of the sensation-creating body.

The Beatles song *Yesterday* remains one of the great paeans to nostalgia and a longing for a return to a simpler and more perfect time in the past. The opening lines suffice to illustrate:

> *Yesterday*
> *All my troubles seemed so far away*
> *Now it looks as though they're here to stay*
> *Oh I believe in yesterday.*
> *Suddenly, I'm not half the man I used to be*
> *There's a shadow hanging over me*
> *Oh yesterday came suddenly.*

The "shadow" which diminishes the former state of wholeness and totality is clearly the ego, the storm cloud that darkens the bright, clear sky of untrammeled consciousness.

Psychoanalysis and Childhood

In the song *Comfortably Numb*, Pink Floyd referred to the idyllic existence we experienced as children, and which has since been long forgotten:

> *When I was a child I caught a fleeting glimpse*
> *Out of the corner of my eye*
> *I turned to look but it was gone*
> *I cannot put my finger on it now*
> *The child is grown*
> *The dream is gone.*

These lyrics lend themselves to interpretation in terms of Freudian psychoanalytic theory. According to Freud, all neuroses and aberrant behavior can be traced back to some form of sexual trauma in early infancy or childhood. The problem facing the psychoanalyst is that of *infantile amnesia*, the fact that the patient's memory does not stretch back to those early days of life, and therefore it is very difficult to unearth these memories in the patient's normal state of consciousness. However, these repressed memories continue to exert a pathological influence on the patient's mental life, and since they are buried in the unconscious they can only present themselves in the distorted forms of dream imagery. The technique of dream analysis can undo the process of distortion, reach back to the underlying childhood trauma, and reveal the origins of the neurosis.[18] In Freud's words:

> It [analysis] also profits from the fact that dreams have access to the forgotten material of childhood, and so it happens that infantile amnesia is for the most part overcome in connection with the interpretation of dreams.[19]

So, returning to the lyrics of *Comfortably Numb* and analyzing them psychoanalytically, the forgotten fleeting childhood glimpse, the vanished dream, refers to a repressed memory which must be discovered by dream analysis, thus dredging up from the unconscious the root cause of the neurosis; this must then be fully experienced by the patient and reintegrated into his consciousness, thus putting him firmly on the path to recovery. The following lyrics by Duran Duran are suggestive of this type of struggle to overcome the pain and trauma of earlier experiences, and to readjust oneself to the appropriate modes of behavior and reaction necessary to survive in the world as a properly functioning member:[20]

> *But I won't cry for yesterday*
> *There's an ordinary world*
> *Somehow I have to find*
> *And as I try to make my way*
> *To the ordinary world*
> *I will learn to survive.*[21]

Footnotes

1. In fact, the retinal surface has a "blind spot" where the optic nerve exits the eye on its way to the brain, and any image which fall on this region is not seen — more evidence that the real nature of the world remains hidden from us.
2. The poem is titled *The Parable of the Blind Men and the Elephant.*
3. Alan Watts, *The Joyous Cosmology: Adventures in the Chemistry of Consciousness.*
4. Bob Dylan, *Chimes of Freedom.*
5. Descartes, *Meditations on First Philosophy.*
6. Jung borrowed the term *archetypes* from St. Augustine. He also correlated the archetypes with Plato's Forms, or *eidola.*
7. C. G. Jung, *Two Essays on Analytical Psychology.*
8. C. G. Jung, *Archetypes and the Collective Unconscious.*
9. C. G. Jung, *The Psychology of Kundalini Yoga.*
10. S. Freud, *Totem and Taboo.*
11. It is worth briefly noting that Nietzsche also spoke of an unconscious mind which projects, via dream images, its contents which have been acquired via millennia of cumulative experience. In his book *Human all too Human,* he wrote:

    > In our sleep and in our dreams we pass through the whole thought of earlier humanity. I mean, in the same way that man reasons in his dreams, he reasoned when in the waking state many thousands of years... The dream carries us back into earlier states of human culture, and affords us a means of understanding it better.

12. C. G. Jung, *The Structure and Dynamics of the Psyche.*
13. Jainism arose in India around the sixth century B.C. Its founder, Mahavira (599 — 527 B.C.), preached a particularly puritanical form of asceticism. His prescribed ascetic practice is summed in the Five Great Vows. Briefly, these are: 1) *ahimsa,* the renunciation of the killing or injuring of all living beings; 2) Renunciation of all vices of untruthful speech arising from anger, greed, fear, or mirth; 3) Renunciation of the taking of all things not given; 4) Renunciation of sexual pleasure; 5) Renunciation of all attachment, small or great, to all things living or non-living.
14. In the Bhagavad Gita, Arjuna was similarly overwhelmed and shaken when Krishna revealed his cosmic, universal form to him.
15. Erich Neumann, *The Origins and History of Consciousness.*
16. Matthew, 18:3. This statement requires further comment. It should not be

misinterpreted as meaning that one should remain in a state of perpetual mental or emotional infancy, refusing to leave the security and comfort of a world ruled by kindly, protective parents, afraid to enter an unknown world ruled by inscrutable and impersonal forces. Jesus urges his followers to become *as* little children, not to remain forever immature and infantile; that is, to rediscover the symbols and archetypes after gaining the maturity and understanding that are *sine qua non* for appreciating them.

17. Recall the earlier discussion of solar and lunar consciousness (in Chapter 2). Solar consciousness is the effulgent light of the Universal Radiance, and lunar consciousness is merely the reflection of that light in the field of *prakriti*, or gross substance.

18. For this difficult task a fair amount of experience and talent is required on the part of the analyst.

19. S. Freud, *An Autobiographical Study.*

20. Although some would argue that adjusting oneself to a world and society that are thoroughly corrupt and manipulative can hardly be considered a cure in any meaningful sense of the word. This theme is discussed in more detail further on.

21. Duran Duran, *Ordinary World.*

1. The cover of Pink Floyd's *Dark Side of the Moon* album

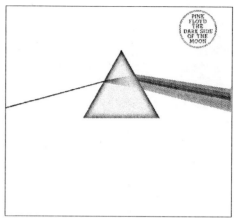

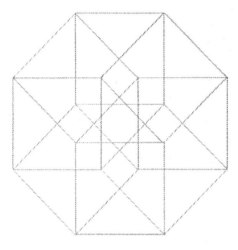

2. Mathematical represen-
tation of a 4-dimensional
hypercube projected onto
3-dimensional space

3. The Chinese Yin-Yang symbol

4. Crucifixion (Hypercubic Body)
(Salvador Dali)

5. Angels and Devils
(M. C. Escher)

6. Diagram showing the seven *chakras*
through which Kundalini energy ascends

7. Setting in which the Bhagavad Gita takes place:
Krishna and Arjuna situated between the two opposing armies

8. God
Separating
Light and Dark
(Michelangelo,
Detail from the
Sistine Chapel)

Obverse   Reverse

9. Above: The Great Seal of the United States

10. Below: Diagramatic representation of various models of the Self

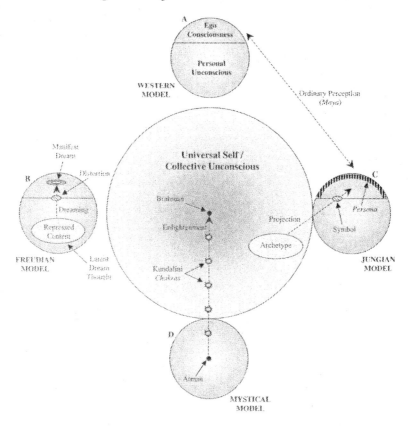

11. Illustration of the Hindu myth of the Churning of the Cosmic Ocean
(Indian miniature painting)

CHAPTER 7

SOCIETY AND THE INDIVIDUAL

If the original state of mind and being was ego-less unity, then something must have been responsible for the disruption of consciousness caused by the ego. One of the reasons for this harmful development has been the baleful influence of society, which has perpetuated this shocking disruption for its own narrow ends. What exactly is meant by "society," and how it creates and maintains the fiction of the ego, will be discussed in greater detail in this chapter.

In a perfectly enlightened age, the driving force behind all human endeavor and undertakings would be the bringing about of the highest moral and spiritual development of its members. Communities would be organized and designed for human ends, to help individuals work in unison towards the aim of activating the higher kundalini *chakras*, thus leading an advanced stage both of civilization and individual awareness. That this sublime state of affairs has not come to pass in most parts of the world, and that what has transpired in its place has been the worst form of perversion of the ideal state, can hardly be a matter of contention. Human concerns have been entirely subjugated to the benighted objectives of an increasingly impersonal and mechanistic society, which uses human beings as pawns in a game that only a privileged few are allowed to play. The ego has been an extremely important player in this sinister game, and so it has been carefully bred and nurtured by the guardians and high priests of the social order.

If the larger human community can be rescued from the clutches of the minority of elite and privileged sectors that have appropriated it for themselves, and if it can be put to work for the common good, then the spirit of knowledge and progress can once again take hold and impel mankind towards its further destination.

The Nature and Function of Society

The cultural, traditional and moral canon of a human collective is enshrined in its society and its institutions. These codes of values and moral principles can be traced to their origins in the traditions, rituals, and philosophical systems of previous generations. The formulation and dissemination of these codes is very often the exclusive jurisdiction of patriarchal structures and groupings, which in rural or traditional societies are embodied in the institutions of tribal elders or the village council. Much of the world still lives under the ethical edicts laid out by early patriarchs and lawgivers such as the Biblical Moses, Confucius of China, and Manu of India. Modern counterparts can be found in the political systems created by the Greek philosophers, which survive to this day throughout Western civilization, and in the founding fathers of America, whose enormous influence on social, political, economic, and corporate structures as they exist today is still strongly felt.

This phenomenon is formally ascribed, in psychoanalysis, to the functioning of the *superego* within the individual. According to Freud, the father's authority over the child is transferred in later life to teachers, society, the Church, etc. These institutions are now invested with the same authority that the father once had over the child, and which now holds sway over the mature individual, because it is internalized and incorporated within him into the formation of the superego or conscience. Thus society, appropriating for itself the authority of the father, via the superego, determines the ideals that a person forms, the values he is guided by, and the standards by which he judges himself and others.

The role of the patriarchy is well illustrated by the Lord's Prayer, below, where the Holy Father is assured that his wishes and injunctions will be obeyed faithfully, and he is beseeched to provide for his followers and to guide them along the proper path:

Our Father

Who art in Heaven

Hallowed be thy Name

Thy Kingdom come

Thy will be done

On earth as it is in Heaven

Give us this day

Our daily bread

And forgive us our trespasses

As we forgive those who trespass against us

And lead us not into temptation

But deliver us from evil.

A person's destiny is seen to be determined exclusively by the heavenly Father, who holds in his hand the ultimate powers of judgment, redemption, and forgiveness. His word is sacred law and is to be unquestioningly accepted.

The larger social or cultural group is a type of surrogate for the divine patriarch, and the individual who belongs to the group is expected to conform to the morality and principles which are largely determined by it, and even to uncritically internalize its values, like an obedient child. Erich Fromm explains why this should be so:

> For all irrational and exploitative forms of authority, self-assertion — the pursuit by another of his real goals — is the arch sin because it is a threat to the power of the authority; the person subject to it is indoctrinated to believe that the aims of the authority are also his, and that obedience offers the optimal chance for fulfilling oneself.[1]

Thus, there is an ongoing conflict between society, which is constantly trying to impose its values and judgments upon its members, and the creative individual who seeks to affirm his or her distinctive personality and to find true self-expression by creating something unique and original. In fact, society attempts to work this situation to its advantage by use of an insidious contradiction, which Alan Watts has termed the *double-bind*, in which the players of the social game are told that they are independent and self-guiding agents, but at the same time they must conform to a strict set of standards and requirements.

The double-bind starts from the earliest stages of life, when children are told not to be copycats, not to do something just because their friends are doing it; in other words, they are to act think and act freely, as the unique individuals that they are. However, even though they are free to act, the outcome of their thoughts and actions *must* be as demanded by society and the family. The child *ought* to love his parents, but this love must be heartfelt and sincere. Further limits on this "freedom" are the bounds of decency, social etiquette, and acceptable behavior, of which society is the purveyor and the judge. In short, the child (and later, adult) is commanded to behave as a free agent, and is told that only voluntary and genuinely spontaneous actions are acceptable, but that all this must occur within a strict and rigid framework of rules, guidelines, and morals. If the person cannot cope with this insoluble antinomy and decides to withdraw from the social game altogether, he will be called an eccentric or a freak, and will be subject to the highest degree of persecution. You are damned if you do and damned if you don't. Bob Dylan alluded to the antagonistic demands of the double-bind in his song, *Maggie's Farm*:

> *Well, I try my best to be just like I am*
> *But everybody wants you to be just like them*
> *They say sing while you slave and I just get bored*
> *I ain't gonna work on Maggie's Farm no more.*

What is the way out of this hopeless quandary? How can one behave in a manner that will be acceptable to others, and yet that is is supposedly spontaneous and voluntary? One way to do this is to disown your own creative self, internalize the ethical standards and mores of your particular cultural ethos, and then deceive yourself that these transplanted values are your very own. You constantly have to forget your real self, and this is nothing less than self-imposed neurosis or schizophrenia, which varies in degrees according to each person. If you are told that $2 + 2 = 5$, and are then commanded to actually *believe* it, some form of insanity has to result. This must, in part, explain the droves of people who today flock to psychiatrists, therapists, emotional counselors, and priests.

When an individual is asked to renounce his deepest and most precious insights, and to submit instead to the system of positive and negative reinforcements maintained by society, these fundamental insights are repressed out of sight. But, as Freud has shown, repressed instincts and thoughts never completely disappear, and in fact often return in ever stronger, distorted and malevolent forms. So, the intuitive mystical undercurrents continue to exert an influence on a person's mental life and, since they are completely at odds with what his outer world has taught and conditioned him to think, they lead to the severe dilemma of the double-bind, the dilemma between that which one knows deep down to be true, and that which one is forced to unquestioningly swallow, like a bitter pill that is supposedly good for you but ends up inducing a feverish delirium.

The other way out of the precarious dilemma is to reject the rules of the social game and listen instead to your own muse, which is by far the more difficult of the options, for then you have the full weight of cultural sanction and tradition against you. This was the option chosen above by Bob Dylan ("I ain't gonna work on Maggie's Farm no more"), who rejected the presumption that society is the most competent judge of what is appropriate and acceptable for all its members, passing down its ordinances from on high like Moses with the stone-engraved Commandments. Dylan advocated instead that each person investigate for himself or herself the merit of all that was being passed off as incontrovertible truth by the self-appointed guardians of the social character and morality. These ideas were compressed into the single, powerful statement: "You don't need a weatherman to know which way the wind blows."[2]

The rejection of uncritical obedience to authority only occurs in the case of the talented, creative, and pioneering individual, who seeks to break out of the shackles tied on him by society. Only the fearless innovator seeks to forge an independent path for himself, unencumbered by the weight of established values. The average, unremarkable individual, on the other hand, requires the shackles and submits willingly to the dictates of the larger order to which he belongs. For him, being a member of a nation, race, or organization provides a feeling of security and a sense of identity and fraternity, without which he cannot deal with the uncertainties and vagaries of a harsh, unforgiving, and unpredictable world.

While analyzing the life and works of Leonardo da Vinci, a fiercely independent thinker and researcher who renounced conventional authority and relied only on his own observation and judgment, Freud confirmed the above statements when he wrote:

> But in teaching that authority should be looked down on and that imitation of the "ancients" should be repudiated, and in constantly urging that the study of nature was the source of all truth, he [da Vinci] was merely repeating — in the highest sublimation attainable by man — the one-sided point of view which had already forced itself on the little boy as he gazed in wonder on the world . . . In most other human beings — no less today than in primeval times — the need for support from an authority of some sort is so compelling that their world begins to totter if that authority is threatened.[3]

Thus, the ordinary individual needs the reassurance and familiarity provided by the moral canon of his collective grouping, and it is the function of the extraordinary individual to define this canon. Nietzsche called this extraordinary individual the "Superman" or higher man, who is the creator of values, and because of his superior will and hardness of spirit he is not bound to any conventions or codes, which exist only for others not endowed with such boldness, strength, and moral courage.

In the imagery of Nietzsche's *Thus Spoke Zarathustra*, the lower man is like the camel that takes upon its back the burden of expectations and edicts piled upon it by society, while the higher man is transformed from a beast of burden into a lion that slays the dragon which has "Thou Shalt" emblazoned on every scale on its body, and which embodies created values that are centuries old. The final transformation of the highest man is into the child, who is "innocence and forgetting, a new beginning . . . a self-propelled wheel." Here we see again the motif of the wheel, representing the original condition of the mind, untainted and uncorrupted by the influence of the world around it.[4] The true creator and discoverer of truths can only go about his task by vanquishing the dragon of "Thou Shalt," by ridding himself of the oppressive weight of society-created values heaped upon him, and returning to the pure, childlike state of freedom from outside influence, prejudice, and memory.

So, the person who has been "bent out of shape by society's pliers," to borrow a phrase from Bob Dylan's *It's Alright Ma (I'm only bleeding)*, must straighten himself out by rejecting accepted norms and forging a new beginning where he is master of his own will, unencumbered by imposed morality and free to create. This is by no means a straightforward task, for the process of indoctrination and ideological molding begins at the earliest stages of the educational process and continues throughout life in almost every field of cultural, social, and economic activity, until society brands its indelible, searing imprint on the individual mind. This institutionalization of the spirit, which in its natural state is irrepressible and boundless, is what Bob Marley urged opposition to when he said:

> *Don't let them fool you*
> *Or even try to school you, oh no!*
> *We've got a mind of our own*
> *So go to hell if what you're thinking is not right*
> *Love would never leave us alone*
> *In the darkness there must come out to light.*[5]

The pressure society exerts on the individual to conform to its traditions and customs was recognized by the Indian thinker and iconoclast Jiddu Krishnamurti, who constantly warned against the dangers of conformity. His emphasis was on observing and understanding the self, and he rejected the authority and influence of social, cultural and political structures in all their forms. Blind, unthinking obedience to the demands of what he considered to be a sick and corrupt society would lead inevitably to a crushing of a person's soul, to an extinguishing of the inner flame of awareness.

Adoption of other people's values and imitation of their behavior and lifestyles can lead only to a false and superficial image of the self which is impossible to live up to, and ultimately can only lead to despair, disillusionment, and feelings of inadequacy. The individualism expressed in the following lines from Jimi Hendrix's *If 6 was 9* is in the same spirit as Krishnamurti's convictions:

> *I've got my own world to live through*
> *And I ain't gonna copy you.*

Before attempting to reform society or the world, Krishnamurti said, it is necessary to transform our own thinking by realizing and understanding the thorough social conditioning that we have undergone. Without this internal revolution of the mind, any attempt at a revolution of the outer world is ill-fated, for it is bound to be contaminated with our prejudices, biases, and preconceived notions. This is what the following lyrics by The Beatles refer to:

> *You say you'll change the constitution*
> *Well you know, we all want to change your head*
> *You tell me it's the institution*
> *Well you know, you'd better free your mind instead.*[6]

Krishnamurti's ideas were taken to chilling extremes by Aldous Huxley in his book *Brave New World*, in which he offered a terrifying glimpse of a future world in which babies are genetically engineered and then conditioned and indoctrinated from the moment of their birth, their whole futures mapped out by the architects of society. This was merely a caricature of what Krishnamurti stated to be, and what most people readily recognize as, real factors operating in society and the world today. The ideological and behavioral manipulation of vast sectors of society by autocratic institutions and highly concentrated power centers in a modern industrialized country like America has been exposed and extensively documented from the period of the early

1960's to the present by Noam Chomsky, Massachusetts Institute of Technology professor of linguistics and long time political dissident.

Society and Ego

Alan Watts has said that the troubles and symptoms from which neurotics, and even normal people to some extent, suffer are inextricably bound up with their relationships with other people, and with the rules regarding these relationships, which are communicated by self-contradictory social and cultural institutions. The psychotherapist, therefore, must understand what the mystics have been saying for thousands of years: that the problems of the individual are not those of an isolated vehicle of consciousness, of a split-off psyche with its private troubles, but that the psyche is thoroughly intermingled with the society, the world, in which it exists. In fact, a person's sense of identity, his feeling of who he is, arises not from the person himself but from other people, from their reactions, demands, and judgments regarding him. Watts writes:

> Other people teach us who we are. Their attitudes to us are the mirror in which we learn to see ourselves, but the mirror is distorted.[7]

The overbearing role of the outside world in the formation of an individual's self-image can not be doubted, because the very terms, images and concepts which constitute all our thoughts were not invented by us, but were handed to us from society. Hence, the problem confronting the psychotherapist is not merely one of individual psychology, but also of how best to liberate the individual from the various forms of social conditioning to which he has been subjected, and which have stunted his normal growth as a fully functional, awake, and alive human being. Watts says:

> The rules of [social] communication are not necessarily the rules of the universe, and man is not the role or identity which society thrusts upon him. For when a man no longer confuses himself with the definition of himself that others have given him, he is at once universal and unique. He is universal by virtue of the inseparability of his or-

ganism from the cosmos. He is unique in that he is just this organism and not any stereotype of role, class, or identity assumed for the convenience of social communication.[8]

He goes further to say that *Maya*, the unreality that must be escaped from, is not in the nature of the physical universe but refers rather to social institutions and the way in which they modify our perception and feeling of the world. The sense of ego, as an invisible presence within the self that observes and controls the feelings, emotions and reactions of the individual, is the principal agent of *Maya* and is an unconscious pretense created by society to manipulate and control its members. As Watts writes:

> When, therefore, I feel that "I" am knowing or controlling myself . . . I should recognize that I am actually being controlled by other people's words and gestures masquerading as my inner or better self. Not to see this brings about utter confusion, as when I try to force myself to stop feeling in ways that are socially objectionable.

> If all this is true, it becomes obvious that the ego feeling is pure hypnosis. Society is persuading the individual to do what it wants by making it appear that its commands are the individual's inmost self.

In this respect, the ego is like a cancerous tumor which arises within the psyche, destroys all the living substance around it and turns the will into a dormant, pliant tool that society can control and direct according to its needs and ends. In Pink Floyd's song *Brain Damage*, which deals with the theme of psychological disorder, the cause of the disorder is attributed to an alien presence inside the lunatic's head which has so completely distorted and mutilated his mind and its functions in an effort to make him "sane," i.e. conforming, that he is incapable of dealing with the confusion and contradiction (of the double-bind), and can only respond by giving up the futile struggle and going mad:

> *The lunatic is in my head*
> *The lunatic is in my head*

You raise the blade, you make the change
You re-arrange me 'til I'm sane
You lock the door
And throw away the key
There's someone in my head but it's not me.

The lunatic in the head is no other than the "ego feeling" mentioned by Alan Watts, instilled and endlessly reinforced by society to
make the individual's actions, thoughts, feelings, and impulses follow a
course that is determined by it.

This relates closely to Jung's concept of the *persona*, which is a sort
of mask that one wears to present a particular picture of the personality to others. The Latin word *persona* was originally used to refer to the
mask worn on stage by an actor in ancient Greece, and it is from this
word that the word "personality" derives. A person has many such
masks, and in daily life he puts on whichever one is appropriate for a
given situation. His personality is different, depending on whether he is
playing with his children, speaking to his boss, addressing a group of
people, and so on. He is simply playing a number of different roles, and
the various masks that he dons throughout life are largely determined
by society. Jung writes:

> Fundamentally the persona is nothing real: it is a compromise be-
> tween individual and society as to what a man should appear to be.
> He takes a name, earns a title, exercises a function, he is this or that.
> In a certain sense all this is real, yet in relation to the essential indi-
> viduality of the person concerned it is only a secondary reality, a com-
> promise formation, in making which others often have a greater share
> than he.[9]

To Thine Own Self Be True

The stultifying effects on creativity of the stipulations and demands of the social order have been understood by many artists and
free thinkers, who have rejected the paths laid out for them by others
and have been guided instead by the Shakespearian adage (in *Hamlet*):

"This above all — to thine own self be true." Without genuine, ongoing creative activity and self-expression there is only spiritual death and decay. To borrow another phrase from Dylan's *It's Alright Ma (I'm only bleeding)*: "He not busy being born is busy dying." The following lines by Erich Fromm make this clearer:

> Birth is not one act; it is a process. The aim of life is to be fully born, though its tragedy is that most of us die before we are thus born. To live is to be born every minute. Death occurs when birth stops. Physiologically, our cellular system is in a process of continual birth; psychologically, however, most of us cease to be born at a certain point.[10]

The world is an extension of the mother's womb, in which we are still contained as embryos, mere germs of possibilities. Endless roads stretch out before us, but first it is necessary to be truly born to our unlimited potential. Only when the tiny flower bud opens up and blossoms in all its iridescent glory does it fully realize its inherent destiny. So too every person remains an incomplete and unrealized work in progress until the creative potential within him or her, according to his/her *dharma* or Tao, has been released and exhaustively employed. Until this is accomplished, one may try to find consolation in conformity, or success, or fame, but nothing can substitute for the process of being continually born to one's higher self. The influence of society is highly inimical to this ongoing act of self-discovery and rejuvenation, a fact that needs to be acknowledged from the outset so that the genuinely creative person knows what he is up against.

Ultimately, the question below posed by Bob Marley is the crucial one, and only those who can embrace it with a life-affirming "Yes" can be said to have found their own *dharma* and liberated themselves from the oppressive dictates of an irrational society:

> *Open your eyes and look within*
> *Are you satisfied with the life you're living?*[11]

Examples abound everywhere of those who cannot honestly answer this all-important question in the affirmative, having been diverted from their purpose by the demands and claims of others. The cities and suburbs are crowded with psychologically half-born, spiritually half-asleep people who do not even know what it means to be really alive, who allow themselves to be manipulated by the world at large, thoroughly unaware of their pitiful semi-somnolent state.

In The Rolling Stones' *Mother's Little Helper*, the subject of the song is an aging housewife exhausted by the thankless duties of looking after an unappreciative family, and for whom "cooking fresh food for her husband's just a drag." In such a life "the pursuit of happiness just seems a bore," and to relieve the otherwise unmitigated tedium of her banal life she finds refuge in prescription pills (the "Little Helper" of the song's title), which she takes in increasingly high doses until it leads eventually to her death. Similarly, the Police song *Synchronicity II* is effectively a harangue against the hollowness of a conformist suburban family lifestyle. In the song, the husband is downtrodden and humiliated at work, stuck in the rush hour traffic hell everyday, his soul deadened to the vitality and energy of life. The lines below, from John Mellencamp's *Jack and Diane*, sum up perfectly the dismal and perfunctory character of such a drab existence where psychic growth has come to a standstill:

Oh yeah, life goes on
Long after the thrill of living is gone.

In the song *If 6 was 9*, Jimi Hendrix derides the corporate executives and businessmen who have relinquished the connection with their creative self, and now feel threatened by the "freaks" who follow their true passions and live their lives as they choose, not as they have been laid out for them by the outside world:

White collar conservatives flashing down the street
Pointing their plastic finger at me
They're hoping soon my kind will drop and die but
I'm gonna wave my freak flag high, high

Go ahead on mister businessman, you can't dress like me.

The recognition here is that the artist and creator is in touch with the fount of imagination and originality deep within the soul of man, and is close to the unconscious and its archetypes, whereas the conforming masses live their blinkered and myopic lives chasing after trivialities, paying no heed to the universal center within them. Remaining oblivious to the divine radiance that emanates from within, they are condemned, in the words of Hamlet, "to grunt and sweat under a weary life." So even though, as mentioned previously, the influence of the unconscious can often be damaging and destructive, sometimes it is preferable to be consumed by it than to lead a passive life, organized and regimented by the decrees of society and authority.

Society and Sanity

The theme of society's stifling influence on the creative, vital energies of life is dealt with in Peter Shaffer's play *Equus*, a psychological study of a boy who has suffered a severe psychosis. In the boy's mind the image of Christ, as he is whipped and tortured on the way to Calvary, has been replaced by Equus, the terrifying horse god whom the boy worships and with whom he communes, in secret, by having orgiastic frenzies at night with horses from the local stable.

While the boy is obviously in need of help, he is at the same time intoxicated with exhilaration and heightened passion in his psychotic state, and Martin Dysart, the doctor who is treating him, reflects on the boy's contact with something vital and energizing, as contrasted with his (Dysart's) own meek, passive, and unadventurous life, sterile and lacking true worship. While the boy is consumed by fervor and devotion to Equus, Dysart is infertile (symbolic of the impotence of his conventional life) and unable to even have conjugal relations with his wife. These excerpts from a speech by Dysart convey the point:

All right, he's sick. He's full of misery and fear. . . But that boy has known a passion more ferocious than I have felt in any second of my life. And let me tell you something: I envy it.

... Without worship you shrink, it's as brutal as that ... I shrank my own life. No one can do it for you. I settled for being pallid and provincial, out of my own eternal timidity ... I sit looking at pages of centaurs trampling the soil of Argos — and outside my window he is trying become one, in a Hampshire field! ... I watch that woman [his wife] knitting, night after night — a woman I haven't even kissed in six years — and he stands in the dark for an hour, sucking the sweat off his God's hairy cheek! Then in the morning, I put away my books on the cultural shelf, close up the Kodachrome snaps of Mount Olympus, touch my reproduction statue of Dionysus for luck — and go off to hospital to treat him for insanity. Do you see?

Conformity and the routinization of life may mitigate the feelings of loneliness and isolation that are the prominent features of the modern age, but these only work by sedating and numbing the mind to its bleak situation. The mind thus numbed, however, becomes not only removed from its sorrows but from its joys as well, and life becomes a meaningless, perfunctory ritual. In a consumer, market-oriented, and technocratic society, anyone who rebels against the norm of a detached and compartmentalized existence where the primary preoccupations are competition and the acquisition of wealth is quite liable to be driven to the edge of insanity and beyond.

It is, however, rarely discussed whether a society itself is sane or insane that does not foster bonds of fraternity, relatedness, unity, and mutual support among its members, but instead forces upon them a Hobson's choice: accept the role that society has defined for you and you will be accepted as a member; reject it and you will be isolated, alone, and ostracized. However, by accepting the role foisted on him by society, a person does *not* overcome his persistent sense of alienation. He simply puts an artificial veneer on it, and compensates for his lack of genuine human relations and creative contact with others by indulging in the various diversions, amusements, and media spectacles that society has ingeniously devised to keep people from dwelling on the gnawing sense of emptiness they feel inside.[12]

By taking part in the rat race of daily existence, it is possible for a person to take his mind off the unbearable alienation threatening to drive him mad, but at what price? Some have found the price of their soul too great a price to pay for acceptance by others and have chosen to withdraw from the world, into their own private fantasies. In other words, insanity within is preferable to the far more horrifying prospect that awaits them outside.

In the song *All The Madmen*, David Bowie voices the feelings of an inmate of a lunatic asylum who refuses to leave the confines of the asylum and join the ranks of the hollow, soulless beings outside its walls:

'Cause I'd rather stay here
With all the madmen
Than perish with the sad men
Roaming free.

From Nurture to Nihilism

It is not inevitable or predestined that society should have the pernicious effects on its members that it does, and indeed some (mainly primitive) cultures have been marked by fraternity, concern for others, mutual support, and a strong sense of community. Unfortunately, the vast majority of modern societies function instead in the harmful and life-thwarting manner detailed by Alan Watts, Krishnamurti, Bob Marley, Bob Dylan, and countless others. Erich Fromm offers some possible reasons as to why this should be so:

> Most of human history (with the exception of some primitive societies) is characterized by the fact that a small minority has ruled over and exploited the majority of its fellows. In order to do so, the minority has usually used force; but force is not enough. In the long run, the majority has had to accept its own exploitation voluntarily — and this is only possible if the mind has been filled with all sorts of lies and fictions, justifying and explaining its acceptance of the minority's rule. However, this is not the only reason for the fact that most of what people have in their awareness about themselves, others, society, etc., is a fiction. In its historical development each society becomes caught in its own need to survive in the particular form in which it has developed, and it usually accomplishes this survival by ignoring the wider human aims which are common to all men. The

contradiction between the social and the universal aim leads also to the fabrication (on a social scale) of all sorts of fictions and illusions which have the function to deny and to rationalize the dichotomy between the goals of humanity and those of a given society.[13]

Even given the corrupt and corrupting nature of the social order, most people have a deep yearning for meaningful, constructive, and productive contact with others in their wider community. The path of the yogi or the mystic is neither possible nor realistic for the large majority of people, and so most visions of a perfect, utopian world do not consist of each person living in a compartmentalized sphere of isolated bliss, but are made up instead of images of universal solidarity and kinship, of people living in peaceful coexistence, where each person encourages and motivates his fellow man to fulfill his creative potential, rather than everyone single-mindedly working in order to hoard goods and possessions merely because society places a premium on any activity that leads to consumption. Such was the vision and hope expressed by John Lennon in the following lines:

> *Imagine no possessions*
> *I wonder if you can*
> *No need for greed or hunger*
> *A brotherhood of man*
> *Imagine all the people*
> *Sharing all the world*
> *You may say I'm a dreamer*
> *But I'm not the only one*
> *I hope someday you'll join us*
> *And the world will be as one.*[14]

As Lennon says, to most people these sound like impossibly idealistic and unattainable fantasies, particularly given the levels of violence, greed, inequality, and exploitation that exist in the world today. However, the fact is that many cultures and societies in the past, and many even in the present day, have come remarkably close to the vision of utopia as it is imagined today. There have been numerous societies that were distinguished by a minimum of hostility and violence, and which were notable instead for cooperation and a nurturing attitude of trust and confidence in others. They were not governed by the principles of control and power because their very functioning depended on the principle of mutuality.

The bane of the modern world is the drive for acquisition. This is not an innate drive, and the reasons for it have much to do with the artificial needs and desires created by society. The level of material possessions required for happiness or contentment is a relative quantity which is in fact largely determined by variable, culturally-conditioned factors. Thus, even though primitive societies had a relatively low standard of living when measured by modern Western standards, there was a high level of relatedness, solidarity and general enjoyment of life which the most advanced technology today has been unable to bring into being. In addition, cooperation and sharing were in fact practical necessities in the hunter-gatherer societies because luck in the hunt or the harvest was unpredictable, and any person might at any time rely on his clansmen to make up for his shortfall. Greed and hoarding were alien concepts for the very reason that they were exceedingly impractical and counterproductive. Thus, there was very little private ownership of land, and all resources were freely shared.

As Fromm has amply demonstrated in his book *The Anatomy of Human Destructiveness*, the popular image today of the primitive man as savage and vicious is a complete misrepresentation of the facts. That early societies relied in part on hunting for their food has been taken as proof of the aggressive and violent nature of pre-civilized man, but there is no evidence to show that the early hunter was motivated by murderous feelings of cruelty or hostility towards the hunted animal. On the contrary, the animal was often regarded as an ancestor or clan member, called "brother" or "father," and honored by totem rites and rituals.

The "fact" of the barbarity of our forefathers is entirely a political and cultural fabrication, and serves as a powerful tool to induce apathy towards injustice and inequality. If it can be shown that human beings were always violent and destructive, then it is easy to infer that they are innately so, and hence that it is futile to raise arms against a sea of troubles, for troubles are the natural condition of the world. All the available evidence, however, shows that primitive man was essentially peaceful and cooperative, and it is the modern, "civilized" man who has shown himself to be the bloodiest and most sadistic creature in history, torturing and slaughtering his fellow man on a scale never before seen.

In the agrarian and hunter-gatherer societies the prime focus of life was food and the few devices necessary for obtaining it, rather than the trappings and accouterments necessary to elevate one's social status. It was very easy to be satisfied with one's lot in life, for modest expectations are easily met. In addition, the primitive lifestyle kept people in fruitful contact with the earth, nature, and animals, with whom a close connection and intimate bond was felt. People had ample time for leisure, art, song and dance, ritual and myth-making, and other forms of creative activity. As Fromm explains, in such a culture the very foundation for inequality and exploitation is lacking:

> Prehistoric hunters and agriculturalists had no opportunity to develop a passionate striving for property or envy of the "haves," because there was no private property to hold on to and no important economic differences to cause envy. On the contrary, their way of life was conducive to the development of cooperation and peaceful living. There was no basis for the formation of the desire to exploit other human beings. The idea of exploiting another person's physical or psychical energy for one's own purposes is absurd in a society where economically and socially there is no basis for exploitation.[15]

This sounds very much like the idealistic picture that John Lennon and countless others have painted of a world at peace with itself. This picture began to change radically, however, after the urban revolution, around the fourth and third millennia B.C. Social organization was now no longer egalitarian and based on neighborly intimacy and camaraderie, but started to become increasingly authoritarian, centrally directed, and under the control of a dominant minority. We now also see the first signs of people leaving their immediate locality to seize raw materials and enslave men from other territories. In short, the aim of culture was no longer the enhancement of life but the expansion of power and influence. Whereas people had previously been relatively self-sufficient, now the emphasis was on private ownership and competition for resources. The division of labor became more marked and rigid, and man was reduced to the status of an economic instrument, a slave to the means of production. The process of the alienation of man from his fellow men was thus set in motion, and the value of human relations significantly lowered.

This process was carried to further extremes in the wake of the industrial revolution, and with the advent of the technological city-state it has now assumed gargantuan proportions. The machine is now exalted above and beyond man, and the focus has shifted alarmingly from living beings to machines, weapons and gadgets. Modern society has effected a complete reversal from the earlier, primitive position, and has succeeded in brainwashing the individual into equating his self-worth and dignity with the sum total of his accumulated goods and properties. A person's intrinsic value is now measured in terms of levels of consumption and material possessions, and on factors totally extraneous to himself, such as the judgments and decisions of the outside world, industry, and the marketplace. Modern advertising successfully hoodwinks the individual into believing that he is only important or worthy to the extent that he immerses himself in the task of consuming and accumulating, to the exclusion of all other activity. As Bob Dylan said:

> Advertising signs that con you
> Into thinking you're the one
> That can do what's never been done
> That can win what's never been won
> Meantime life outside goes on
> All around you.[16]

Thus, it is the new age of materialism and cutthroat competition that has caused man to feel estranged, isolated, and cut-off from others, and it is the lack of human relations that has turned him into a sadist, torturer, and killer. Any attempt to impute these factors to innate characteristics or inherent tendencies of the human species is merely a disingenuous attempt to deflect the blame away from their true cause — always and again, society.

The expansiveness of life and *joie de vivre* have been severely cur-
tailed, and this blockage of spontaneity and expressiveness has serious
repercussions. These include a pathological state of alienation from the
outside world, and a lack of human emotion inside. In severe cases this
leads to a sense that one is not entirely human, and to a feeling of doubt
whether one is even capable of feelings — nihilism, in the most pessimistic and negative sense of the word, a dispossession of one's basic
humanity. The lyrics below, by Nine Inch Nails,[17] attest to this feeling
of emptiness and deadness within:

> *I hurt myself today*
> *To see if I still feel*
> *I focus on the pain*
> *The only thing that's real.*[18]

Erich Fromm also detailed some clinical case studies he had come
across in hospitals and in a boys' training school; they are very relevant
in this context, for they deal with thoughts and acts that correspond
closely to the above lyrics. The following extract describes two such
cases:

> One girl, hospitalized in a state mental hospital, had slashed her
> wrists and explained her act by saying that she wanted to see if she
> had any blood. This was a girl who felt nonhuman, without any re-
> sponse to anyone; she did not believe she could express or, for that
> matter, feel, any affect. (Schizophrenia was excluded by a thorough
> clinical examination.) Her lack of interest and incapacity to respond
> was so great that to see her own blood was the only way in which she
> could convince herself that she was alive and human.

> One of the boys in the training school, for instance, threw rocks up on
> top of his garage and let them roll down, and would try to catch each
> rock with his head. His explanation was that this was the only way in
> which he could feel something.[19]

Something must be terribly wrong with a society that strips its
members so completely of their humanity and vitality that they resort
to self-mutilation in order to "feel something," even if that something

should be agony. It is indicative of a massive failure on the part of a community which allows such pessimism and gloom to become widespread, and which does not place a premium on the spiritual health of all members. It also explains the high incidence of sadomasochism in modern cultures. Deep down inside man still longs for a feeling of relatedness and unity with others, but this aim is not consistent with the goals and directives of society and so it remains repressed and unfulfilled. Denied a healthy and creative expression, this aim is perverted into a sadistic expression. Sadism is also a form of relatedness to others, but by means of domination and control. Also, total control over another helps to alleviate the feelings of powerlessness and helplessness engendered by an exploitative social order.

Every person contains within him/herself the caged beast, the dark angel — what Jung termed the *shadow*. In individual cases the beast may break free as the result of a psychosis, but for this to happen on a large scale requires deep-seated and endemic cultural factors. Modern technocratic society, with its accentuated and overemphasized duality between man and environment, provides fertile soil for breeding such mass psychoses.

In the second period of his life's work, Freud postulated that life is a battlefield where two grand passions are locked in interminable conflict. These are the "life instinct," or Eros, and the "death instinct."[20] The life instinct encompasses such life-furthering drives as hunger and sexual appetite. The death instinct, when it is directed inward against the organism itself, becomes self-destruction or self-negation, and when it is directed outwards it destroys others. It is not difficult to judge which of the two instincts predominates today. What little doubt remains can be removed by looking at the following lyrics by The Rolling Stones, which could hardly have surfaced in an environment that promoted life and growth:

> I see a red door and I want it painted black
> No colors anymore I want them to turn black
> I see the girls walk by dressed in their summer clothes
> I have to turn my head until my darkness goes

I look inside myself and see my heart is black
I see my red door and it has been painted black
Maybe then I'll fade away and not have to face the facts
It's not easy facing up when your whole world is black.[21]

Freud has said that God is nothing other than a projected father-figure, and also that in adulthood the authority of the father is transferred to societal and religious institutions. When faith in these institutions as providers of security, wholeness, and cohesion is lost, then belief in a benevolent, just, and kind God is also shattered. This helps to explain the Nine Inch Nails' vituperative outburst in the song, *Heresy*:

Your God is dead[22]
And no one cares
If there is a hell
I'll see you there.

How is the world to be rescued from such raging negativity? There has been much public outrage and protest over such bands as Nine Inch Nails and Marilyn Manson, as well as heavy metal and death metal bands, and others who promote violence, death, and necrophilia. However, the real cause for concern is the number of young people who flock to these bands and regard them as articulators of their own inner frustrations and disillusionment. Anger and despair do not arise in a vacuum, and these artists are merely reflecting the ubiquitous sense of hopelessness which is the inevitable outcome of the commodificaton and devaluing of human life and existence. If God is dead, then man cannot be far behind.

To resurrect both God and man, society must be made a model and expression of man's innermost needs, desires, and longings, but what we have in fact is the reverse: man as a tool for manipulation by society according to *its* requirements. A person's time at work is controlled and directed by the industry for which he is working, and his recreation time is directed by the industries of entertainment and leisure. There is really not a moment's respite from the unceasing onslaught of corpo-rate-industrial values. The modern era has made money, wealth, greed, and conformity the new totem symbols around which everyone gathers and salutes, paying homage to the new plastic gods and creeds. When love, beauty, and kindness are treated as just another in a long line of commodities waiting to be packaged, shrink-wrapped and sold, little room remains for the flowering of the human spirit, just as a delicate rose can hardly be expected to bloom when it is hemmed in by thickets of barbed wire. Don Henley described the situation wonderfully in the following lines:

> These times are so uncertain
> There's a yearning undefined — people filled with rage
> We all need a little tenderness
> How can love survive in such a graceless age?
> The trust and self-assurance that lead to happiness
> They're the very things we kill, I guess
> Pride and competition cannot fill these empty arms
> And the work I put between us doesn't keep me warm.[23]

Moral and spiritual well-being can be thought of as the ability and freedom to be fully creative, active, responsive, and awake, but the modern lifestyle of television, advertising, and intense competition in all aspects of life is hardly conducive to the nurture of such construc-tive and vivifying tendencies. When the *esprit de corps* is supplanted by ruthless egotism, it reduces the individual to a passive spectator, an impotent and disempowered onlooker mutely observing what goes on all around, lacking the power or even enthusiasm to take an active role in the dynamic process that is life.

This pathetic state of society and culture is all the more tragic be-cause of the vast potential they have for uniting people into a cohesive and supportive organic structure. Ample evidence exists to show that few things are more difficult for the average man to bear than the feel-ing of not being identified with a larger group. Erich Fromm has noted that often people go to war to experience the feeling of camaraderie with others, for in the war or battlefield situation all discrimination based on class, creed, and socio-economic status is temporarily suspended. The nature of warfare is such that all the participants are engaged in a life-or-death struggle, and therefore the most capable and competent are the most highly valued. Rather than staying home and suffering prejudice and oppression, many opt for military service, where they will be treated as equals and judged on merit alone.

The need for communal acceptance and belonging is so strong that a person will often seek the approval and approbation of his society even when it is thoroughly ruthless and depraved. A case in point is that of Nikolai Bukharin, who was a leading figure in the Soviet Union during the Bolshevik revolution and beyond, and in many ways outshone dictator-to-be Joseph Stalin in economic policy decisions and intellectual contributions to party ideology. Bukharin, however, soon met his doom in the terror of the Stalinist purges of the 1930's. He spent years languishing in prison, and had to make humiliating confessions before being finally executed. He recognized Stalin and his regime for the monstrosities that they were, right from the beginning, but even as he witnessed the atrocities and brutality all around him he could not bring himself to betray his party in order to win a reprieve from his fate. Bukharin eventually confessed to the most outlandish and fantastic crimes that were fabricated against him, even though he knew that it would lead to his death. A speech he made before his execution explains his reasons for doing so:

> There was nothing to die for, if one wanted to die unrepentant . . . And when you ask yourself: "Very well, suppose you do not die; suppose by some miracle you stay alive, again what for?" Isolated from everybody, an enemy of the people, an inhuman position, completely isolated from everything that constitutes the essence of life.[24]

All organisms have an inherent tendency to actualize their specific potentialities, and the aim of man's life is therefore to be understood as the unfolding of his unactualized powers and energies, his complete humanization. A truly progressive and humanistic society will recognize and encourage these tendencies, for a person is more likely to succeed in his aim if he has the reassuring knowledge that others too have the same longings as him and that he has in them a mutual and reciprocating support base with which he can work towards common goals. This support base was very much present at some point in the past, before the drive for wealth and power became overbearing, and there is no reason that it cannot be made so again. For this to happen, the individual must first liberate himself from the crippling double-bind, and then assist others in doing the same. Only by working in concert and in conjunction can people reclaim the future for themselves by winning freedom for creative expression and activity, and by laying the basis for a humane, egalitarian, and sane society. This parallels the way of mysticism, which seeks liberation from within rather than waiting for it to be granted from above. The following lyrics by Bob Marley say it all:

Emancipate yourselves from mental slavery
None but ourselves can free our minds.[25]

Footnotes

1. Erich Fromm, *The Anatomy of Human Destructiveness*.
2. Bob Dylan, *Subterranean Homesick Blues*.
3. S. Freud, *Leonardo da Vinci and a Memory of His Childhood*.
4. In Chinese philosophy this unadulterated state is designated by the term *p'u*, which means an uncarved block, one that has not been cut or shaped, i.e. which has remained untouched by the outside world and hence maintained its purity.
5. Bob Marley, *Could You Be Loved*.
6. The Beatles, *Revolution*.
7. Alan Watts, *The Book: On The Taboo Against Knowing Who You Are*.
8. Alan Watts, *Psychotherapy East and West*.
9. C. G. Jung, *Two Essays on Analytical Psychology*.
10. Erich Fromm, D. T. Suzuki, and Richard de Martino, *Zen Buddhism and Psychoanalysis*.
11. Bob Marley, *Exodus*.
12. As Noam Chomsky has pointed out, the fact is that an isolated, diverted, and cut-off human being is much easier to indoctrinate and manipulate than one who is engaged in meaningful, productive, and stimulating contact with his fellow man. This fact has not been lost on those in power, who have an inordinate amount of influence and control in the shaping of society, especially in today's world of mass media and entertainment. The person who is estranged from others is less likely to organize with them to work towards eliminating the concentration of wealth and unequal distribution of resources which are responsible for the misery of much of the world, but which work very much in favor of the prosperous few.
13. Erich Fromm, D. T. Suzuki, and Richard de Martino, *Zen Buddhism and Psychoanalysis*.
14. John Lennon, *Imagine*.
15. Erich Fromm, *The Anatomy of Human Destructiveness*.
16. Bob Dylan, *It's Alright Ma (I'm only bleeding)*.
17. Nine Inch Nails is one of a new breed of contemporary bands dealing, in frequently graphic and disturbing words and imagery, with the disaffection and dehumanization created by the grim facts of modern society.
18. Nine Inch Nails, *Hurt*.
19. Erich Fromm, *The Anatomy of Human Destructiveness*.
20. The word *Thanatos* is often used for the death-instinct, but Freud himself

never used this term.

21. The Rolling Stones, *Paint It Black*

22. This is obviously highly suggestive of Nietzsche's famous "God is dead" statement in *Thus Spoke Zarathustra*. It also interesting to take a slight diversion and consider this line in regard to a hypothesis put forward by Freud in his *Totem and Taboo*, in which he related the sacrifice of Christ on the cross to unconscious murderous fantasies towards the father, which is one half of the Oedipus complex. Freud wrote:

> There can be no doubt that in the Christian myth the original sin was against God the Father. If, however, Christ redeemed mankind from the burden of original sin by the sacrifice of his own life, we are driven to conclude that the sin was a murder. The law of talion, which is so deeply rooted in human feelings, lays it down that a murder can only be expiated by the sacrifice of another life: self-sacrifice points back to blood-guilt. And if this sacrifice of a life brought about atonement with God the Father, the crime to be expiated can only have been the murder of the father.

23. Don Henley, *The Heart of the Matter*.

24. Quoted in: Alan Bullock, *Hitler and Stalin: Parallel Lives*.

25. Bob Marley, *Redemption Song*.

CHAPTER 8

EXPANSION OF CONSCIOUSNESS

.

The Infinite Mind

In preceding discussions it has been shown that the collective unconscious, or Universal Soul, is infinite in expanse, and only a fraction
of it can be experienced by the weak and limited conscious mind of an
individual. Some have proposed that the reason the human mind is confined to perceiving only a minute portion of the whole of reality is actually for its own protection. It is simply not equipped to deal with the
universe in its full, undimmed glory, and would be shattered by the
sheer magnitude of it, just as the naked human eye cannot directly look
into the glare of the blazing sun, and would be blinded if it did.

This was the view put forward by the French philosopher Henri
Bergson (later elaborated by Cambridge philosopher Dr. C. D. Broad),
about which Aldous Huxley wrote in *The Doors of Perception*. Bergson
contended that the function of the brain is not productive, but is, on
the contrary, eliminative. What he says is that it is theoretically possible for any given individual to have in his possession universal knowledge, i.e. to remember everything that has ever happened to him in minute detail, and to have full cognizance about all the events happening
everywhere in the entire universe. However, the mind would be completely overwhelmed by the sheer volume of this information and
would be annihilated. Therefore, the function of the brain, nervous sys-

167

tem, and sense organs is to act as a filter and reduce the amount of information that is passed to the mind to a level that the mind can cope
with.

Sri Aurobindo said much the same thing, and he identified the
reductive function as *Maya*. He wrote:

> Infinite consciousness in its infinite action can produce only infinite
> results; to settle upon a fixed truth or order of truths, and build a
> world in conformity with that which is fixed, demands a selective
> faculty of knowledge commissioned to shape finite appearance out of
> the infinite reality.

> This power was known to the Vedic seers by the name of maya. Maya
> meant for them the power of infinite consciousness to comprehend,
> contain in itself and measure out, that is to say, to form — for form is
> delimitation — name and shape out of the vast illimitable truth of
> infinite existence. It is by maya that static truth of essential being
> becomes ordered truth of active being.[1]

The true nature of the universe and our self is infinity, but our fee-
ble minds are incapable of apprehending this infinity and so it must be
broken up into manageable chunks for us, just as we must reduce our
food to manageable mouthfuls before we can digest it. As a result, infinity is reduced to localized space, and eternity is attenuated to measur-
able time, with our brains acting as the reducing valve or funnel that
causes this diminishment. If the reducing valve is bypassed, then everything is seen in its untrammeled totality. In the words of Blake:

> If the doors of perception were cleansed every thing would appear to
> man as it is: Infinite.

> For man has closed himself up, till he sees all things thro' narrow
> chinks of his cavern.[2]

The Bhagavad Gita as well says: "When one sees Eternity in
things that pass away and Infinity in finite things, then one has pure
knowledge." The following lines from the Tao Te Ching also seem to

concur with the view that universal knowledge is latent within every individual:

One may know the world without going out of doors.
One may see the Way of Heaven without looking through the windows.

Knowledge of the world and heaven lie untapped within each individual, and that which is perceived through the windows of the eyes and the senses is but an infinitesimal fragment of the totality.

It is worth recalling here the parable of the blind men and the elephant, discussed previously. The six blind men were unable to apprehend the elephant in its entirety, and consequently formed a wrong impression of it based on the small portions that they were able to directly grasp with their hands. This is also what Gestalt psychology suggests; namely, that the whole is greater than the sum of its constituent parts, and that each of the parts, if taken in isolation, leads to a completely invalid interpretation of the whole. Given that the brain acts to break up the whole into smaller pieces, individual components are all we are ever presented with and so the holistic view eludes us.

The Destructive Unconscious

As discussed earlier, the unconscious mind is almost universally represented in mythology by deep waters, the ocean, the fathomless abyss, etc., and a plunge into these waters is a descent into the depths of the unconscious. Given that it is a crucial function of the brain to reduce the flow of this primordial ocean, psychological mechanisms must be in place which act as a dam, checking and holding back the torrential flood of the infinite ocean, only allowing through a small trickle. Any failure of these mechanisms would result in a mass of unconscious, archetypal material surging into a consciousness that is incapable of assimilating it, and would lead to a total collapse of sanity. The Pink Floyd song *Brain Damage* deals with just such a breakdown of psychological functioning. It too employs the imagery of a dam bursting, of insufficient capacity to restrain the unleashed deluge, and the consequent collapse into insanity:

And if the dam breaks open many years too soon
And if there is no room upon the hill
And if your head explodes with dark forebodings too
I'll see you on the dark side of the moon.

The dark side of the moon, here, symbolizes the dark recesses of the mind where the afflicted person is imprisoned and tortured by the uncontrollable forces of his psyche. A similar convergence of the themes of water and of being destroyed by the immensity of unconscious forces appears in the following lines from Dylan's *Maggie's Farm*:

I wake up in the morning
Fold my hands and pray for rain
I got a head full of ideas
That are driving me insane.

After being overwhelmed by the onrush of unconscious material engulfing his mind, the sufferer cries out for these forces to subside and for a return to sanity. His salvation lies in the dissipation outwards, into cathartic rain, of the flood that submerged and swallowed him. This was the method originally used by Freud in treating cases of neurosis by hypnotic methods, which he termed the *cathartic technique*. It involved the release of dammed-up psychic energy (*libido*) which was being misdirected and causing the damage, and the channeling of this energy along the normal path of discharge (*abreaction*).[3]

The opening lines of the song *Sway*, from the towering Rolling Stones album *Sticky Fingers*, reveal an understanding of the potentially disintegrating effect of the unconscious on the personality. In these lines a scenario is presented of a sudden collapse of normal mental processes, and the subsequent regression into terrifying regions of the unconscious:

Did you ever wake up to find
A day that broke up your mind
Destroyed your notion of circular time
It's just that demon life has got you in its sway.

Here the delicate psychological homeostasis that supports the fragile facade of sanity has been shattered, and the hitherto proscribed forces of the destructive side of the personality have broken through. The demons and apparitions of the psyche that had thus far been kept in check by complex psychological structures and mechanisms have broken through to consciousness and overrun it completely, destroying its normal perceptions and functions. With the failure of these protective mechanisms, the mind sinks back into the primordial abyss, where it is annihilated and all contact with the outer world is severed.

The serious risk of this type of a breakdown is what led Jung to constantly warn people from the West not to dabble with yoga, for it unleashes powers and energies that are wholly alien to them, and which they are completely ill-equipped to handle. This is because the Western character is almost exclusively extroverted, i.e., it is concerned with the intellect, consciousness and the exterior world, and so it is at a total loss when confronted with mysterious unconscious forces to which it has never given proper consideration. Its psychic orientation is completely different from that of the introverted East, which developed yoga according to its own internal needs and realities. Just as the tongue and stomach rebel against exotic foods, so the mind rebels against being remolded according to alien and exotic concepts.

Therefore, while yoga practices can help Westerners to expand the scope of their consciousness, it can do nothing to help them assimilate the often terrifying thought-figures and hallucinatory visions that stream out from the unconscious and enter the newly created opening in the mind. The Eastern yogi, on the other hand, because of his introverted character, can understand these figures as empty and insubstantial forms whose looming presence effectively blots out the divine light behind them from undeserving eyes. The true master can depotentiate them and deprive them of their illusory power (*maya-shakti*). Once the demons have been recognized for the hollow shapes that they are, they become translucent and the pure light that they were shielding comes bursting through. If, however, one believes in the concrete reality of these apparitions, the result is a complete mental or schizophrenic collapse.

The East has always been oriented towards the unconscious and has spent thousands of years developing and refining techniques to plumb its depths and subdue the *makara*[4] that is to be found there. The necessary spiritual conditions have been created in the Orient such that yoga is a wonderfully appropriate and invaluable technique for uniting mind and body, consciousness and unconscious, and thereby achieving perfect wholeness. However, Jung said, the unwitting Westerner whose outlook and mentality have been conditioned almost exclusively by exterior circumstances and outward-directed goals (wealth and fame) should not take yoga too far, for he will eventually find himself confronted with the terrible sea-monster, which he will mistake for reality and against which he does not stand a chance, with the result that the unity of his consciousness will be destroyed. The mental state which is the loftiest and most cherished, to the Eastern yogi, can lead to severe mental imbalances when induced in the Western man. Jung writes:

> The deliberately induced psychotic state, which in certain unstable individuals might easily lead to a real psychosis, is a danger that needs to be taken very seriously indeed. These things really are dangerous and ought not to be meddled with in our typically Western way. It is a meddling with fate, which strikes at the very roots of human existence and can let loose a flood of sufferings of which no sane person ever dreamed.[5]

Jung therefore advocated that the West develop its own system of yoga, one that is based on a religious and philosophical approach that is specifically attuned to the Western mindset and that will enable it to decipher in the most appropriate way the arcane and enigmatic symbols of the self. According to him, this Western yoga will almost certainly have to be founded on Christian principles.

Knowledge of the cultural/historical foundations of one's conscious orientation and perspective are essential if the personality is to be kept whole and balanced, for a person cannot simply bathe in the waters of Lethe and reforge himself into something completely different and unrecognizable. To ape a philosophy or spiritual technique that runs contrary to one's background and psychic constitution is akin to thoroughly uprooting a tree and attempting to re-plant it in a location where the soil and climate are entirely unfavorable. Only by tracing and following the origins of his mind does a person pursue the best path to a full appreciation of his inmost identity. As Bob Marley sang:

If you know your history
Then you would know where you're coming from
Then you wouldn't have to ask me
Who the hell do I think I am.[6]

Mystic and Hallucinatory Visions

Many people have made the observation that the visions and hallucinations described by schizophrenics correspond to a remarkable degree with mythological images and patterns, and with the revelations described by mystic seers of the fourth dimension. This is because the plethora of images originates from a common region of the human mind: the collective unconscious. There is, however, a crucial difference between the schizophrenic or psychotic person, and the yogic master. The master has entered the mystical depths by expanding the scope of his consciousness through various mechanisms such as psychophysical (yogic) training, breath control, and mental discipline, and in this state of higher consciousness he is able to withstand the devastating invasions from the unconscious and to assimilate its terrifying images. The schizophrenic, however, is uninitiated and has been thrust into this yawning chasm through a mental or neurological disorder, where his consciousness is now disastrously overtaken by forces beyond its power to control or subdue. He is out of his mind, whereas the yogi is beyond mind. Joseph Campbell explains it thus:

What is the difference between a psychotic or LSD experience and a yogic, or a mystical? The plunges are all into the same deep inward sea; of that there can be no doubt. The symbolic figures encountered are in many instances identical. . . But there is an important difference. The difference — to put it sharply — is equivalent simply to that between a diver who can swim and one who cannot. The mystic, endowed with native talent for this sort of thing, and following, stage by stage, the instruction of a master, enters the waters and finds he

can swim; whereas the schizophrenic, unprepared, unguided and un-
gifted, has fallen or has intentionally plunged, and is drowning.[7]

In *All the Supermen*, David Bowie sings about an earlier age of the
world, when a breed of supermen walk the earth, masters of the spirit
who have trained and strengthened their minds to open up and receive
the vision of universal oneness. The lines below talk of those supermen,
and also about the lesser mortals, ravaged by the very same vision because of their lack of training and mental capacity:

> *Where all were minds in uni-thought*
> *Power weird by mystics taught*
> *No pain, no joy, no power too great*
> *Colossal strength to grasp a fate*
> *Where sad-eyed mermen tossed in slumber*
> *Nightmare dreams no mortal mind could hold.*

Here again we have the symbolism of water ("mermen"), and of
insufficient capacity to keep at bay the abounding forces of the unconscious ("Nightmare dreams no mortal mind could hold"), which suggests that the "sad-eyed" imagery refers to oppression under a mental
disorder, along the lines just discussed.

All of the concepts, formulations and symbolisms discussed so far
in the present context are elegantly integrated in the Hindu myth of the
descent to earth of the sacred river Ganga (or Ganges). In the story, the
earth is suffering under a terrible drought and the mighty river goddess
is summoned from her heavenly abode and asked to descend to earth,
and so provide it with much-needed water. However, a serious problem
presents itself at this point because the sheer force that would be
unleashed by the cascading waters from the heavens would be too great
for the earth to bear, and it would be pulverized. To solve this problem,
Shiva agrees to absorb the initial impact of the water by trapping the
deluge in his hair, from where it then trickles down to earth with a
much-reduced force.

Thus, if we identify Ganga in this myth with the infinite scope of
universal knowledge, Shiva with the reductive function of the mind,

and the earth with individual consciousness, we have perfect harmony between the psychological theory of Bergson, the observations of Campbell, and Hindu mythology, as well as the music of Pink Floyd, Bob Dylan and David Bowie.

It is interesting to note that Jung's discovery of the archetypes came about in large part due to a particular case of schizophrenia that he encountered.[8] The case in point was that of a man in his thirties, who had at one time been employed as an ordinary clerk. He became ill in his early twenties and began suffering from severe hallucinations and delusions of being the Savior. One day when Jung went to see him, the patient told him that if he looked at the sun with eyes half shut, he could see the phallus of the sun. And, if he moved his head from side to side, the sun-phallus would move as well, and that this was the origin of the wind. At the time this made little sense to Jung, but when he later came across a study dealing with a liturgy of the ancient cult of Mithras, it all fit together. The study contained a series of instructions and visions, one of which was of a tube hanging down from the sun disc, the direction of which dictated the movement of the winds. This was a striking parallel, particularly since the patient had been committed some years before that particular study had been published, so that even the slightest possibility that he might have been influenced by a reading of it could be safely discounted.

Furthermore, in many medieval Christian paintings, the wind-tube is shown as a sort of pipe in which the Holy Ghost travels to impregnate the Virgin Mary, so the phallic symbolism of the patient's vision is also accounted for by a mythical motif. The recurrence of these basic themes from such disparate and independent sources as a modern-day schizophrenic hallucination, an obscure Mithraic liturgy, and medieval Christian symbolism, led Jung to the conclusion that these ideas have always existed (in other words, they are archetypes), and can be found in the most diverse minds in all ages (that is, they are contained in the collective unconscious). In the case of the patient, madness was the outlet and outcome of these raw, unmodulated supra-individual forces, which in the other cases had been properly modified via ritual and art before being brought to the surface.

The Use and Effects of Psychedelics

The use of psychedelic and psychotropic substances to induce states of enhanced and expanded consciousness is as old as human culture itself, and these substances have often been used as sacraments in religious rites and ceremonies. The shamans of ancient Mayan civilization made liberal use of the psilocybin mushroom, a particularly potent hallucinogen which produced visions of paradise and was, furthermore, known for its healing powers. In the sacrificial ceremonies of the Vedic religion of India, one of the oldest in the world,[9] the sacred *soma* juice was offered to the gods and then distributed among the human participants as a libation that conferred immortality and divine inspiration upon its drinkers. It is now generally accepted that the *soma* juice was extracted from the plant *Amanita muscaria*,[10] a mushroom whose juice is poisonous in full strength, but hallucinogenic and intoxicating when diluted with milk, water, or honey.

For two thousand years in the village of Eleusis, in ancient Greece, a ceremony was held annually which involved the use of a psychedelic concoction known as *kykeon*, a beverage believed to contain barley ergot.[11] Almost every prominent figure in Greece was initiated into the Eleusinian Mysteries, including Socrates, Plato, Aristotle, and Sophocles. All who had participated in the ceremony were forbidden to speak about it, on pain of death, but still reports about the happenings leaked out. People talked about seeing luminous, ineffable visions in which all divisions melted into a single dazzling light, and of realizing that the beginning and end of life are the same event.

In addition, there are innumerable other cases of primitive and tribal cultures using sacred mushrooms, cacti, and other psychotropic forms of vegetation as sacraments in their ceremonies and rituals. In more recent times, perhaps the most famous self-experiment regarding the effects of mind-altering drugs has been Aldous Huxley's *The Doors of Perception*, in which the author details the vivid impressions and thoughts he experienced after consuming 400 milligrams of peyote, or mescaline. In *The Joyous Cosmology: Adventures in the Chemistry of Consciousness*, Alan Watts recounted the transcendent and deeply mystical insights afforded to him after partaking of various quantities of LSD.

Also, Timothy Leary, Terence McKenna, and R. Gordon Wasson have been outspoken proponents of controlled psychedelic use, and have written large bodies of work advocating the use of psychedelics for augmenting consciousness, and even as therapeutic aids in combating various forms of depression and addiction.

Rock and roll musicians, in particular, have been notorious for their use of consciousness-altering substances, and no doubt a not-insignificant number of the insights and mystical intuitions of the musicians discussed in this book have resulted directly from their partaking of psychedelics. In fact, an entire era of music is known as the "psychedelic 60s," mainly due to the influence that LSD, marijuana, and other psychoactive substances had on the *zeitgeist* in the 1960s.

The rationale and spirit behind the taking of these psychotropic chemicals has been to experience, via an alteration in the chemistry of the brain, those realms of thought which lie hidden and inaccessible to us in the "normal" state of mind. Psychedelics assist greatly in overcoming the resistances, inhibitions, and divisions that are inherent in the neurological constitution, and those which are enforced by society. Therefore, the changes in thought and perception that arise have often been compared with those produced by religious fervor and mystical exultation. In fact, the descriptions people offer of their pharmacologically-enhanced inner journeys past the barriers within the self are often virtually indistinguishable from passages taken from classical mystical texts, just like the schizophrenic visions discussed in preceding pages. Furthermore, psychedelic drugs and plants are often referred to as *entheogens*, which means "becoming the God within," or "the realization of God within one's own self."

The use of entheogenic plants as divine sacraments has its (diluted) counterparts in the Christian faith. The ancient Aztecs worshipped a sacred mushroom which they called *teonanacatl*, "the flesh of God;" when it was eaten, the deified Spirit of the mushroom entered into the body. Compare this with the Christian doctrine of Transubstantiation that underpins the use of bread and wine as sacraments of the Eucharist. The doctrine proclaims that in Holy Communion the bread and wine are transformed into the body and blood of Christ. The bread and wine of the Eucharist are merely placebo sacraments, inactive symbols of the primordial element, whereas imbibing the *teo-nanacatl* produces an activé and vibrant experience of the desired communion. Like the Greeks, the Aztecs and Mayans kept the divine entheogen a jealously guarded secret, for fear that it would be profaned or desecrated by those who were not ready to be initiated into its secrets.

The goal of inducing acutely heightened states of consciousness has been pursued by countless people throughout history, for they have recognized that the standard mode of sensing, apprehending, and thinking is but one among others. In the *locus classicus* on the subject, the American psychologist William James wrote:

> Our normal waking consciousness, rational consciousness as we call it, is but one special type of consciousness, whilst all about it, parted from it by the flimsiest of screens, there lie potential forms of consciousness entirely different. We may go through life without suspecting their existence; but apply the requisite stimulus, and at a touch they are there in all their completeness, definite types of mentality which probably somewhere have their field of application and adaptation. No account of the universe in its totality can be final which leaves these other forms of consciousness quite disregarded.[12]

But what is the "requisite stimulus" that will tear down this "flimsiest of screens" and bring about knowledge of the "universe in its totality"? Yoga and meditation are definitely techniques that can bring about this alchemical transformation of the mind, but they require years of rigorous training and discipline. Psychoactive drugs provide an expedient alternative. Just as the microscope is an artificial mechanism for observing the minuscule world of microbes and bacteria, and the telescope is an artificial mechanism for observing the remote world of planets and stars, so the hallucinogen can be considered an artificial mechanism for direct observation of the undiscovered universe within the self. These artificially induced paranormal experiences open up expansive vistas beyond the horizons of this life, and bring to light phantasmagoric images that would be otherwise destined to remain obscured from us. The following lines by The Doors unambiguously mention charting undiscovered realms of consciousness, on which one has not as yet made landfall:

Let's swim to the moon
Let's climb through the tide
Surrender to the waiting worlds
That lap against our side.[13]

Some are of the opinion that by dissolving boundaries and erasing differences, psychedelics provide a chemical key to unlock the doors of perception, as it were, to open out the gates leading to a lost continent within the human mind, and to the discovery of new modes of thinking, seeing, feeling, and a radically new way of being — the mystic way. The reason for the almost identical character of the psychedelic and the mystic vision is that they both result after the frontiers of the known are reached, beyond which one then hurtles into astral regions of uncharted consciousness. This new world looks sparklingly pristine and new, and one melts in the radiant glow of its overwhelming beauty. The interference of the mortal eyes is suspended, a tremendous feeling of openness radiates through the mind, and one sees, in the words of Blake, "a world in a grain of sand."

The number of songs in rock and roll dealing with the psychedelic experience are too numerous to e examine exhaustively within the scope of this book, and so only a couple of them will be used here as examples. The first is Jimi Hendrix's *Purple Haze*, which depicts the initial unsettlement that one feels when directly confronted for the first time with sensations that are beyond the bounds of rational thought. Like climbing a mountain or charting the seas, it takes time to master the psychedelic universe and come to terms with the dislocation of thought, sense, and feeling that occurs there. Old habits die hard. However, once consciousness shifts to adjust to the new sensations, they are correctly interpreted and can be traced to their roots in the unmanifest world, the unconscious, within which reside the transcendent intuitions of eternity and infinity. The following lines reflect all these various shades of meaning:

Purple Haze
All in my brain
Lately things just don't seem the same

Acting funny, but I don't know why
'Scuse me, while I kiss the sky

.

.

.

Purple Haze
All in my eyes
Don't know if it's day or night
You've got me blowing, blowing my mind
Is it tomorrow, or just the end of time?[14]

In the writings of Plato we find the same mystical notion of an originally timeless world, onto which the processes of time have been imposed by an interfering ego. This original world, like the submerged Atlantis of the mind rediscovered by Hendrix through his pharmacological aids, is described by Plato below:

> For there were no days and nights and months and years before the heaven was created, but when he [the creator] constructed the heaven he created them also. They are all parts of time, and the past and future are created species of time, which we unconsciously but wrongly transfer to the eternal essence.[15]

The Beatles song *Lucy in the Sky with Diamonds* is a description of a kaleidoscopic LSD experience, in which all perception has been distorted and magnified.[16] The following extracts from the song portray a wholly transmogrified consciousness:

Picture yourself in a boat on a river
With tangerine trees and marmalade skies
Somebody calls you, you answer quite slowly
A girl with kaleidoscope eyes
Cellophane flowers of yellow and green
Towering over your head
Look for the girl with the sun in her eyes
And she's gone.   .

Newspaper taxis appear on the shore
Waiting to take you away
Climb in the back with your head in the clouds
And you're gone.

It is a fact that LSD, psilocybin mushrooms, *soma*, et al., often produce vivid hallucinations.[17] But the case can be made (as it has been by
Alan Watts) that the state of ordinary sobriety, with its lack of awareness of the basic unity of all life and consciousness, is the severest and
most harmful hallucination of all. In fact, Timothy Leary is reputed to
have said: "Psychedelics often produce psychotic and even violent behavior in those that have never used them."

An important distinction needs to be drawn between the properties and effects of psychedelics such as LSD, mescaline, and marijuana,
and those of narcotics such as heroin, amphetamines, and barbiturates.
All of these are usually bundled together without discrimination under
the general rubric of "drugs," and the average person is most likely unaware of the differences between them. But the differences are great.

Some people maintain that the available evidence shows that if
psychedelics are taken in the correct dosage and in moderation, there is
little likelihood of physiological or neurological damage. They produce
little or no physical craving, and indeed those who take them are so
overawed by the experience that they hesitate to approach the next
dose until the previous one has been fully appreciated and digested.
Toxic drugs such as heroin and cocaine, on the other hand, are addictive poisons which have a devastating effect on physical and mental
health. Intoxicants such as alcohol and opium greatly dull the senses
and induce a state of stupor, as opposed to the hallucinogens, which
heighten and sharpen the senses and make them more sensitive to impressions.

This is not to say that psychedelics are risk-free or that they can
be treated flippantly. There is much that is unknown about their effects
on the body. Certainly, they may be harmful when taken in excess or in

impure form. However, similar considerations have not deterred people from using penicillin, anesthetics, sedatives, and the like. Just as sophisticated medical technology, with known potential risks and side-effects, is used to remove cancerous tumors within the body, so the malignant tumor that is the ego can be removed from the psyche with pharmacological assistance. Sometimes people have reported panic while under the effect of a hallucinogen, and this is usually related to the loss of the sense of ego, which most people cleave to dearly. As was mentioned when discussing the Great Void within the self,[18] loss of ego in the unenlightened state is usually associated with the death of the organism, and so sometimes people report terrifying sensations of being near death or of melting away into nothingness. For this reason, advocates of psychedelics have always qualified their statements with a cautionary warning that these substances are not to be trifled with, and are to be taken only in a balanced mental state that is conducive to the correct appreciation of the new experience. Anybody who is mildly psychotic or paranoid is likely to be pushed over the edge. Almost all the dangers of entheogens are mental rather than physical, and they require a certain level of preparedness and openness for what is to come if they are to lead to a genuine mystical unfolding of consciousness.

To minimize the risk of such frightening episodes, proponents of psychedelic experimentation (such as Alan Watts and Timothy Leary) have recommended that the experiments be conducted in a comfortable, supportive, and preferably naturalistic setting. Furthermore, a qualified and sympathetic medical practitioner should be on hand to oversee the proceedings, someone who can be called upon to provide a reassuring point of contact with "reality," if it should be needed. This usually eliminates the elements of anxiety and paranoia which can lead to harrowing experiences while the drug is in effect, and almost all people who take psychedelics in these relaxed and secure circumstances report positive and enlightening experiences as a result.

So, what is the reason for the taboo against psychedelics, a taboo which does not extend to such harmful and addictive substances as alcohol and tobacco? Watts has offered a most interesting suggestion regarding this. Since the psychedelic experience has such a strong affinity with the mystical one, it tends to lay great emphasis on the union between God and man, on the identity between Brahman and Atman.

However, viewed through the eyes of Judeo-Christian theology, this amounts to the preposterous and sacrilegious assertion that every single person is God made manifest in the flesh. The Christians insist that this was true only in the unique instance of Christ the Savior, and for anyone to claim this divinity for himself is outright heresy. As Watts says:

> If, in the context of Christian or Jewish tradition, an individual declares himself to be one with God, he must be dubbed blasphemous (subversive) or insane. Such a mystical experience is a clear threat to traditional religious concepts. The Judeo-Christian tradition has a monarchical image of God, and monarchs, who rule by force, fear nothing more than insubordination. The church has therefore always been highly suspicious of mystics, because they seem to be insubordinate and to claim equality or, worse, identity, with God.[19]

Therefore, if a chemical or plant incites droves of people to claim identity with God, it is hardly to be wondered at that this inducer of mass heresy and insubordination should meet with the strongest opposition from the orthodox religious establishment, who see it as a direct challenge to cherished traditional shibboleths.

We turn now very briefly to some secular reasons for opposition to psychedelic drugs. As discussed previously, any factor, chemical or otherwise, which reduces a person's willingness to play the hypocritical social game, and which produces indifference to the manipulative system of encouragements and dissuasions set up by society, is not likely to endear itself to the power centers and institutions within that society. When a person sees the futility and absurdity of worldly ambition; of being merely a consumer of corporate products; of the delirious craving for material success and fame; of television, luxury cars, strip malls, weekend sports, and the like, and therefore refuses to join in the ludicrous charade, he will more likely than not be referred to as "antisocial" or "subversive." He then runs a greater than usual risk of ending up in a mental institution or correctional facility of some sort. His real crime is that he has not allowed himself to be subjected to the surreptitious forms of behavior modification and conditioning that are the principal functions of most types of societally condoned activities, pursuits, and recreation. By not participating in these activities, he removes himself from the public arena and hence from exposure to the various forms of social conditioning and hypnosis which democratic societies so heavily depend on, for they do not have recourse to the methods of outright violence and subjugation by force that totalitarian societies can rely upon.

In John Carpenter's 1988 movie *They Live*, a race of aliens has inhabited the earth, but to all outward appearances they look completely human. They ensure obedience from the human population by encoding unseen, subliminal messages such as "Obey" and "No Independent Thought" on advertising boards and in magazines, and "This is your God" on dollar bills. Only by wearing specially designed sunglasses do these hidden messages become visible, and the aliens seen in their actual extra-terrestrial appearance. It does not require a great leap of imagination to identify the aliens in the movie with real-life political and corporate elite nuclei of concentrated wealth and power, and the subliminal messages with the subtle, and not-so-subtle, pressures to consume, conform, and cooperate. It only requires the special sunglasses to expose the hidden subtexts for what they are. It is perhaps not coincidental that in the movie these glasses are called "Hoffman lenses" and that the inventor of LSD was Albert Hoffman.

The larger issues of the legalization and legitimization of psychedelics are too complex to go into here, but suffice it to say that the most addictive and lethal narcotic known to man, which has killed more people on the planet than any other known drug, is perfectly legal and is in fact freely available and distributed globally — namely, tobacco.

Drug Abuse and Psychic Inflation —
The Velvet Underground's Heroin

The sinister side of drug use is the abuse of addictive and noxious drugs such as heroin, cocaine, and alcohol, which have extremely harmful effects on the body and the mind over the course of time. These toxins gradually corrode the spirit and the flesh, and generally leave desolation and despair in their wake. Many a prodigious talent has been laid to waste by such substances, and the number of rock stars who have either died from drug overdoses or have had to endure years of torturous dependency on them is staggering.

The Velvet Underground's (that is, Lou Reed's) song *Heroin*, is one of the great epic masterpieces of rock and roll. It describes the harrowing journey into the soul of a heroin addict, where the initial elation of the heroin rush eventually gives way to complete devastation. It also portrays the baleful aspect of undisciplined and reckless inflation of consciousness, and so it serves as an appropriate counterbalance to the preceding discussion of psychedelic mind expansion.

The song begins with a sparse, minimalist, almost dirgeful instrumental and vocal arrangement, which for a while alternates with surges of tempo, each successive surge representing the administration of a dose of heroin. The opening lines speak of a sense of despair and loneliness, and out of the depths of this darkness the spirit cries for deliverance:

> *I don't know just where I'm going*
> *But I'm gonna try for the kingdom, if I can*
> *'Cause it makes me feel like I'm a man*
> *When I put a spike into my vein*
> *And I'll tell you, things aren't quite the same*
> *When I'm rushing on my run*
> *And I feel just like Jesus' son*
> *And I guess that I just don't know*
> *And I guess that I just don't know.*

The reason for taking heroin is, here, the same as it is for most people who use psychedelics, namely to "try for the kingdom," that is, to leave behind the drabness of life and arrive at the organic and unitary vision of the universe the mystics speak of. While the initial rush of heroin does produce a heightened perception, what follows is a rapid downward spiral into bodily and spiritual debasement caused by the toxicity of the drug.

At the peak of its effect, heroin produces feelings of almost divine grandeur ("I feel just like Jesus' son"). Consider the following hymn from the Rig Veda, which is similar in some respects to Lou Reed's dark litany:

We have drunk the Soma; we have become immortal; we have gone to the light; we have found the gods. What can hatred and the malice of a mortal do to us now, O immortal one?[20]

The difference is that the Vedic hymn is exuberant and exultant because it results from a psychedelic reduction of ego so as to offer a glimpse of the eclipsed, unknown self, whereas the exaggerated self-image engendered by heroin soon collapses ("And I guess that I just don't know") because it results from a process diametrically opposed to the Vedic one — namely, from a dangerous expansion of ego such that it seizes hold of the mind and refuses to admit anything else into it. All assessments of self-worth become bound up with this inflated estimation of oneself, and once this estimation proves to be unfounded the crash to reality is all the more horrific — the bigger they come, the harder they fall. This is a phenomenon that Jung has termed *psychic inflation.*

According to Jung, psychic inflation generally results from the extension of consciousness, and it occurs whenever people are overpowered by knowledge or by some new realization. When a weak ego or consciousness arrogates to itself the domain that belongs to the unconscious, this leads to a misguided sense of one's importance and powers, an assessment divorced from reality. The ego becomes enormously inflated, and megalomaniac delusions often arise. The consequences of such overestimation of the self are usually drastic, and when the balloon of false grandeur finally bursts (due to the effects of *enantiodromia*) the ego comes crashing to earth, all the more pitiful for its fallen state.

The previously analyzed myths of the Garden of Eden and the Promethean fire-theft can also be seen as references to instances of psychic inflation, of conscious acquisition of knowledge that was properly the dominion of the unconscious, with terrible consequences for the presumptuous transgressors — Adam and Eve expelled forever from Paradise, and Prometheus chained to a lonely crag in the Caucasus, forsaken by God and man.

The bruising return to reality is demonstrated even more clearly in the Greek story of Icarus, whose father, Daedalus, fashioned wings with feather and wax that would enable them both to escape from the labyrinth in which they were imprisoned. Icarus' wings enabled him to soar effortlessly in the sky, but he became intoxicated with his new-found power and, with his inflated hubris, flew too near the sun, which melted the wax in his wings and sent him plummeting down to the sea, where he drowned.

A similar type of inflation can be seen in Jimi Hendrix's above-quoted "'Scuse me while I kiss the sky" metaphor from *Purple Haze*,[21] which professes a belief in superhuman powers or prowess. If taken literally, such a belief can be dangerous. One needs to be in complete control of the latent psychical powers that the chemical agents tap into, otherwise they completely deluge the ego and cause the conscious will to wilt like a sapped flower. U2 provides this word of caution:

> *If you want to kiss the sky*
> *Better learn how to kneel.*[22]

This is the crucial qualification that prevents psychic inflation from exacting its awesome toll. Kneeling usually implies a humbling, and in this case it implies a reduction of ego. This deflation, as it were, ensures that the psychedelic experience leads to an expansion of the mind and self in their totality, not merely of the ego or top-level consciousness (as is the case with heroin).

The song *Heroin* continues:

> *I have made the big decision*
> *I'm gonna try to nullify my life*
> *'Cause when the blood begins to flow*
> *When it shoots up the dropper's neck*
> *When I'm closing in on death*
> *And you can't help me now, you guys*
> *And all you sweet girls with all your sweet talk*
> *You can all go take a walk*
> *And I guess that I just don't know*
> *And I guess that I just don't know.*

Now the truly menacing and life-thwarting aspects of the addiction have started to come to the fore. Everything is sacrificed to the thrill of the momentary rush, and the imagery begins to takes on a foreboding tone. Reed professes that he has made the conscious decision to dive headlong into the dark abyss, knowing full well that by doing so he is abdicating his claim to his very life and spirit. Furthermore, he is retreating into a place of terrible loneliness and sadness, beyond the reach of human contact. He abjures not only himself but all relationships and emotional bonds with his fellow man.

After another verse, in the lull following the increase of tempo that accompanies each heroin jolt, we hear the first sustained buzz of electronic feedback in the song, heralding the physical and emotional damage wrought by the drug. Bleakness is now the dominant motif, and the lyrics become overtly morbid, reflecting the barrenness of a soul that is attracted like a moth to the flame in which it knows it will be immolated. It continues:

Heroin, be the death of me
Heroin, it's my wife and it's my life
Because a mainer to my vein
Leads to a center in my head
And then I'm better off and dead
Because when the smack begins to flow
I really don't care anymore
About all the Jim-Jim's in this town
And all the politicians making crazy sounds
And everybody putting everybody else down
And all the dead bodies piled up in mounds.

The feedback is now raised to fever pitch, the tempo of the song and the pounding of the drums grows ever faster and more urgent, culminating in a crescendo of emotion and frenzied rush of manic energy. The heroin is now completely in control, and the intensity of the shrieking feedback testifies to the destruction the drug causes as it ascends to the brain, tearing at the fabric of the soul and the flesh, spreading its poison. Over this terrifying, cacophonous, and starkly beautiful soundscape of purgatory, Reed intones the requiem for the mortally wounded psyche:

'Cause when the smack begins to flow
Then I really don't care anymore
Ah, when the heroin is in my blood
And that blood is in my head
Then thank God that I'm as good as dead
Then thank your God that I'm not aware
And thank God that I just don't care
And I guess I just don't know
And I guess I just don't know.

The descent into nihilistic doom is complete. The drums fall silent, but the screeching feedback continues. The moribund spirit has lost all its original vitality and vigor; this is spiritual death. The tragic fall from the initial euphoria of psychic inflation to the negation of life itself has played itself out, and it is a sickening, shattering conclusion. Where there once was a vibrant, pulsing core of potential energy within consciousness there is now only a hollow shell, "more dead than alive," to borrow a phrase from another Lou Reed song dealing with heroin (The Velvet Underground's *I'm Waiting For The Man*). These are the horrors of narcotics abuse, where each fix is one lurch closer to the edge of the precipice, with damnation waiting below. As Nietzsche said: "If you gaze long into the abyss, the abyss gazes also into you."

Footnotes

1. Sri Aurobindo, *The Life Divine.*
2. William Blake, *The Marriage of Heaven and Hell*. It is from these words that Huxley chose the title of his book *The Doors of Perception*, and from which in turn Jim Morrison chose the band name *The Doors*. The lines below from The Door's song *The End* clearly reveal the influence that Huxley's book had on Morrison:

   Can you picture what will be
   So limitless and free.

3. In fact, when Freud later developed his theory of repression, he switched the emphasis of therapy to uncovering and confronting these repressed memories, and correspondingly changed the name of his technique from *catharsis* to *psychoanalysis*, a term which has since been universally employed.
4. Recall the discussion of kundalini yoga in Chapter 3, where it was shown that before any expansion of consciousness can take place, the second *chakra* in the ascent of kundalini energy must be mastered. This is the chakra of the unconscious, represented by water, which contains within it the *makara*, the leviathan or sea monster, which must be overcome before the higher *chakras* of illumination can be reached.
5. C. G. Jung, *Psychological Commentary on "The Tibetan Book of the Dead."*
6. Bob Marley, *Buffalo Soldier.*
7. Joseph Campbell, *Myths to Live By.*
8. The details of this case are to be found in: C. G. Jung, *The Structure and Dynamics of the Psyche.*
9. The coming of the Aryans, the founders of the Vedic system, to India is generally dated around 1500 B.C.
10. Much of the research that led to this discovery was conducted by R. Gordon Wasson, and was detailed by him in his book *Soma, Divine Mushroom of Immortality.*
11. Ergot is the fungus that was used by Albert Hoffman in his 1938 invention of lysergic acid diethylamide, better known as LSD.
12. William James, *The Varieties of Religious Experience*
13. The Doors, *Moonlight Drive*
14. Jimi Hendrix, *Purple Haze*
15. Plato, *Timaeus*
16. John Lennon denied that the song was inspired by a psychedelic episode,

and instead claimed that he wrote it after seeing a painting made by his son. However, the surrealistic and hallucinatory quality of the song is undeniable, and the fact that the initials of the main words in its title spell "LSD" did little to dispel the rumors.

17. Much emphasis been laid on the seeing of brightly colored images and moving shapes under psychedelic influence, but these serve to distract from the real potential of the experience, which is not centered on such trivial amusements, but on a real and profound mystical transformation.

18. See Chapter 4, under the heading *Ego Dissolution and The Great Void*.

19. Alan Watts, *Psychedelics and Religious Experience*. This article originally appeared in the *California Law Review* in 1968.

20. *Rig Veda, 8.48.3.* Translated by Wendy Doniger O'Flaherty.

21. C.f. the "head in the clouds" imagery in The Beatles' *Lucy in the Sky with Diamonds*.

22. U2, *Mysterious Ways*.

PART THREE

THE HERO JOURNEY

CHAPTER 9

THE CALL TO ADVENTURE

The Inward Journey

The guiding principle of the mystical tradition is that the ultimate aim in life is to attain pure knowledge through total experience of the reality that lies beyond the senses is — not abstract, intellectual knowledge of this reality, culled from books or by other indirect means. Therefore, a heavy emphasis is placed on mental training, discipline, and mastery of the body, which are necessary to achieve the goal of union with the divine; and, correspondingly, the accumulation of knowledge and facts is eschewed as worthless — a diversion from the real task at hand. Thus the Tao Te Ching says:

Abandon learning and there will be no sorrow.

And:

In ancient times those who practiced Tao well
Did not seek to enlighten the people, but to make them ignorant.

This is because the knowledge that has been instilled in the individual from birth is compounded of the greatest lies and deceptions,

195

and increasing this knowledge does not lead to enlightenment but simply increases one's ignorance and error. Instead of vicarious knowledge, what is needed is direct, immediate understanding and awareness of the inner reality underlying all outward, external appearances. This is, of course, the most difficult of tasks, and the mental acuity required for it is only achieved after great discipline and sacrifice. Don Henley very aptly describes the task at hand and the tremendous mastery of will needed to discard ideas acquired over a lifetime, as proposed by the Tao Te Ching, and to view everything afresh with a sense of child-like wonder:

> The more I know, the less I understand
> All the things I thought I knew, I'm learning again
> I've been trying to get down to the heart of the matter
> But my will gets weak and my thoughts seem to scatter.[1]

It can well be imagined that attempts at laying aside one's thoughts and ego will initially meet with the greatest frustration, but like all worthwhile endeavors it requires properly directed persistent effort. If done correctly, it will lead to the Zen-like state where thought itself is transcended in a blaze of *satori* and the pure Self shines forth in its universal splendor, unobstructed by thought and knowledge. In the Kena Upanishad we read that the immanent Spirit makes itself known thus:

> He comes to the thought of those who know him beyond thought, not to those who imagine he can be attained by thought. He is unknown to the learned and known to the simple.

So, the true seer renounces the worldly sphere and works for his salvation by delving into the depths of his being and finding the answer to the age-old question of existence within his own heart. Joseph Campbell has termed this inward journey the "hero journey," and in his seminal book *The Hero with a Thousand Faces* he proposed a mythic schema for the archetypal journey of the hero figure. In all mythologies, the hero goes through three stages in his process of transformation from an average person into an enlightened being who has overcome the delusion of the senses. Broadly speaking, these three stages are: 1) separation, 2) initiation, and 3) return. In Campbell's own words:

> A hero ventures forth from the world of the common day into a region of supernatural wonder; fabulous forces are there encountered and a decisive victory is won: the hero comes back from this mysterious adventure with the power to bestow boons on his fellow men.[2]

In contemporary music, also, these stages are alluded to, although they are depicted differently and are colored by the governing idiom of the prevailing culture. What should be borne in mind is that the journey or adventure is always inwards, directed towards the self, and is undertaken to reveal the hidden world beyond the seen and the known. The Svetasvatara Upanishad describes the undertaking of this inward journey:

> With upright body, head, and neck lead the mind and its powers into thy heart; and the OM of Brahman will then be thy boat with which to cross the rivers of fear.

The realm now being entered is that of the unconscious, far removed from the familiar world of the waking state, and since this is the realm from which dreams and myths originate, the landscape and the forces which the hero encounters are tinged with a magical, supernatural glow. Campbell says:

> Hence the incidents [of the mythic journey] are fantastic and "unreal": they represent psychological, not physical, triumphs. Even when the legend is of an actual historical personage, the deeds of victory are rendered, not in lifelike, but in dreamlike figurations. . . The passage of the mythological hero may be overground, incidentally; fundamentally it is inward — into depths where obscure resistances are overcome, and long lost, forgotten powers are revivified, to be made available for the transfiguration of the world.

Precisely such a transfigured dream-world is portrayed in Led Zeppelin's Tolkien-influenced *Ramble On*. The song opens with a restless hero, embarking upon a night journey into strange lands, and preparing for the adventures that lie ahead:

The leaves are falling all around
Time I was on my way
Thanks to you, I'm much obliged
For such a pleasant stay
But now it's time for me to go
The autumn moon lights my way
For now I smell the rain and with it pain
And it's heading my way.

Plato's allegory of the Cave, which he laid out in *The Republic*, portrays the difference between the ordinary and the heroic. The situation in the allegory is as follows. A group of people lives in an underground cave with their hands and feet chained, and their backs to a fire which is the only source of light, so that all they see are flickering shadows of themselves and other objects. They do not realize the limited and unreal nature of the life they are living, and mistake the shadows for substance.[3]

Then one of the prisoners is freed and goes outside to the world of light for the first time in his life. At first, he is unable to stand the glare of direct sunlight and is blinded, but gradually he begins to see things as they really are, in the clear light of day. He realizes then the completely false notion of the world that he had when he was imprisoned in the cave, and his consciousness is altered forever by the direct knowledge of things, not merely of their shadows. Plato then reveals the meaning of this tale: the underground cave is the world which all of us experience through the senses, and the person who escapes its confines is the enlightened adventurer who ascends to the highest summit of the soul.

In these allegories and tales, it is understood that the journey involves many dangers, and that the path upon which the hero embarks is strewn with perils. All of the mythological heroes had to meet and conquer formidable monsters and adversaries before the fair maiden or the treasure that lay beyond them could be won. The world of the unconscious is not to be trifled with, and can only be experienced by the talented and the initiated. The dilettante will not progress far down the path before being defeated.

The myths and folk tales of the world abound with demons and other fearsome creatures prowling in the dark, beyond the known world, waiting to devour the unwary traveler who has ventured too far from the confines of his society. The fears, apprehensions, and delusions instilled in this manner serve to dissuade the unwitting would-be victim from stepping out of bounds, and to protect him from powers within the psyche (of which he has no inkling and which will destroy him if unleashed). Only the true hero can conquer his fear, steel his will, vanquish the terrible forces that stand in his way, and lift high the priceless treasure that he has won.

The indomitable spirit of independent self-discovery was articulated by The Who in the following lines:

> *Nothing gets in my way*
> *Not even locked doors*
> *Don't follow the lines that been laid before*
> *I get along anyway I care*
> *Anyway, anyhow, anywhere.*[4]

Discontentment and Separation

The first stage of the hero journey is to separate from quotidian life and embark upon the great adventure. The opening lines of U2's *Where The Streets Have No Name* talk about the desire to escape from the confines and limitations of the ordinary world, a world which sounds very much like the description of Plato's Cave above:

> *I want to run*
> *I want to hide*
> *I want to tear down the walls*
> *That hold me inside*
> *I want to reach out*

And touch the flame
Where the streets have no name

I want to feel sunlight on my face
See that dust cloud disappear without a trace
I want to take shelter
From the poison rain
Where the streets have no name.

Just as the hero in Plato's myth saw the fire of the sun for the first time, here too the goal is to "touch the flame" and feel the "sunlight on my face." Once the dust clouds darkening the mind are dispelled, names and labels lose significance and all things can be apprehended in their unadorned glory, shorn of their superficial trappings.

The craving for adventure is characterized in rock and roll by the romantic and charismatic figure of the rebellious loner who is not tied down to any particular person or place, and who is constantly on the move. The classic example of this type of characterization is Steppenwolf's *Born To Be Wild*, which begins with the words:

Get your motor running
Head out on the highway
Looking for adventure
And whatever comes our way.

This song was used prominently at the beginning of the movie *Easy Rider*, as two free-spirited bikers speed down a highway, traveling from one end of the country to the other on their motorcycles. The movie in fact deals primarily with people who have broken from conventional, mainstream society and have formed an alternative lifestyle; essentially, they embody freedom. This break from society and embarking on the uncertain voyage is the basic feature of the first stage of the hero journey.

In rock and roll music, the call to adventure takes the form of a restlessness of spirit, a yearning for adventure, and a reluctance to be confined, restrained, or attached in any way. The individual must be absolutely free to pursue his destiny, unfettered and unencumbered by attachments and obligations, just as the monk, Zen master, or yogi must be free from greed, passions, and desires in order to realize his universal self. In *Stone Free*, Jimi Hendrix sings:

> *A woman here, a woman there, try to keep me in a plastic cage*
> *But they don't realize it's so easy to break*
> *But sometimes I can feel my heart kinda running hot*
> *That's when I've got to move before I get caught*
> *And that's why you can't hold me down*
> *I don't want to be tied down*
> *I've gotta be free.*

Similarly, in Led Zeppelin's *Ramble On*:

> *Got no time for spreading roots*
> *The time has come to be gone*
> *And though our health we drank a thousand times*
> *It's time to ramble on.*

In a more subtle way, the following lines from Zeppelin's *Stairway To Heaven* speak of the haunting allure of magical lands and realms, calling like a siren song from within the soul:

> *There's a feeling I get*
> *When I look to the west*
> *And my spirit is crying for leaving.*

The first step on the adventure of the spirit is a feeling of discontentment with the status quo, with the unremarkable life of everyday experiences, and a desire to explore new frontiers. Without the craving for something beyond the mundane and familiar, no adventure and no discovery is possible. The perils are great, but the reward is greater than anything previously imagined: a vision of our true selves, as proclaimed by the mystics and prophets. To turn away from the journey is to remain trapped in Plato's cave, an intolerable situation for the seeker of truth — of whom The Rolling Stones said:

Don't question why she needs to be so free
She'll tell you it's the only way to be
She just can't be chained
To a life where nothing's gained
And nothing's lost
At such a cost.[5]

The voice that calls from within urges us to leave behind our dreary lives, our preoccupation with the commonplace, and to discover ourselves anew, as we really are. It tells us to transform our life as we know it, and thus become illumined with the glow of knowledge that can only be obtained by plunging into the depths of the unknown, by plucking the watercress of immortality from the floor of the primordial ocean, as in the Babylonian myth of Gilgamesh. The watercress exists within us; we just need the courage to dive in and recover it. The adventure calls to everyone, but only few have the resolve to answer and to take the fateful plunge.

Descent into the Deep

The first step in the hero journey is to answer the spirit's call to adventure, and not to shirk one's destiny. For, to be sure, the decision to embark upon a journey fraught with danger is not an easy one to make. In almost all the tales of heroes, adventurers and warriors, the central character must survive the harshest trials, endure harrowing travails, and battle terrifying creatures. Only after the various monsters and demons that try to thwart the progress of the hero have been slain does he attain the treasure that he seeks. And the treasure is always glorious — the elixir of immortality, a beautiful princess, jewels and riches beyond compare. The demon forces that the hero must slay represent the desires, fears, hopes, and resistances that exist within every person, and which must be overcome before the treasure is won. Winning the treasure is symbolic of liberation of the self from the confines of the flesh, and its absorption into the all-permeating soul matter which supports the universe.

Like the mythological figures such as Odysseus, Theseus, and Gilgamesh, the savior figures of religion, such as Jesus, Buddha, and Mohammed, also went through trials and tests of spiritual courage before discovering within themselves the source and center of all the worlds. Jesus spent forty days in the desert, where he was tempted by Satan. Mohammed retired to the hills near Mecca when he first had the intimation of his messianic calling, and there underwent a revelatory experience when an angel from heaven spoke directly to him. The Buddha had to endure the full might of the fury of Kama-Mara (Love and Death) before attaining Nirvana. In the revered Hindu epic *The Ramayana*, the divine king Rama had to live in exile in the forest for fourteen years and kill the demon Ravana, who had kidnapped his wife, before he could ascend the throne that belonged to him and wear the crown that was rightfully his.

None of the figures in myth or religion had an easy road to the supreme goal, but then the rewards attained by them were of such magnitude and significance that they were not to be bestowed upon unworthy men incapable of the inner strength and sacrifices necessary for the hero journey. It is clear that, in this journey, brute strength and physical endowments are immaterial; what is required is courage of spirit and clarity of perception.

Going down into the underworld cave, the limitless sea, purgatory, and the like, are all metaphors for the test of mental fortitude; the hero must prove himself capable of mastering his fears and moving forward. The mind guards its secrets jealously and does not easily offer them up into daylight, for what is contained within its deepest center is too potent to be meddled with by the novice, as we have seen. This is the reason that, in mythology, the entrance to the cave is almost always guarded by a dragon or some other threatening creature.[6] The real identity of this dragon is revealed in David Bowie's lyrics,

> I ran across a monster who was sleeping by a tree
> And I looked and frowned and the monster was me.[7]

The guardian that is blocking the gate is the ego, the sense of "I" which is projected by the unconscious, and it is this which must be vanquished. The hero/mystic must first be a dragon slayer, and for this he must sacrifice all that he has and all that he believes he is. Ego-death clears the way for a new birth, the birth of the spirit out of matter. However, it has been amply demonstrated that letting go of all the desires, hopes, and ideas that have been inculcated from birth is the sternest challenge that man can face. Most people choose to turn away from this challenge and therefore to remain in an infantile spiritual condition, safely cocooned in the familiar and predictable fold of their society, which serves as a sort of second, ersatz womb, in which a person never really gestates to full maturity.

The strength of will required for this great emotional upheaval is unlike anything that has been demanded of us before; from where can we summon the resolve to put the torch to the house in which we grew up, and which is invested with all our memories of childhood? The heart quivers and the hand trembles, but only after all the old paths and ways have been demolished does the second birth (perhaps even more important than the first, physiological one) take place, so that the distilled spirit can rise like the phoenix from the ashes of the old blundering and groping self. In the following lines, The Rolling Stones spoke of the emotional tsunami that must be weathered before consciousness is incarnated in its fully actualized avatar:

> Faith has been broken, tears must be cried
> Let's do some living after we die.[8]

For the ancient Egyptians, the process of death and resurrection was personified by the scarab, or dung beetle, which they worshipped as khepri, the sun-god. The beetle pushes a ball of dung across the earth; and after it buries the ball in the ground, newly-hatched beetles creep out (the invisible larvae having been implanted there). It is thus a symbol of the self-begetting sun, which sinks into the bowels of the earth every night and resurrects itself anew at the break of every dawn. In this way the scarab is also a living manifestation of self-renewal out of base matter.

The culmination of the hero's adventure is reached when finally the obstructing and threatening forces that block his way have been defeated, and the treasure has been obtained. As with the story of Gilgamesh, the treasure is often hidden within the depths of the ocean, or the belly of some great sea monster. It was noted earlier that the ocean is very commonly used as a metaphor for the unconscious, the concealed soul, and is represented in kundalini yoga by the waters of the *svadisthana chakra*. The monster who swallows the hero alive is the *makara* associated with the *svadisthana chakra*, and corresponds to the dragon guarding the cave. Only by fathoming the dark, uncharted waters of the infinite ocean, and successfully confronting the behemoth lurking within, can the treasure of enlightenment and salvation be won.

In the Arthurian legend, King Arthur received Excalibur, the divine sword that conferred royalty upon him, from the bosom of a lake. In the Bible, Jonah originally rejected the task that God demanded of him, and only after being swallowed by the whale did he see his error, repent, and embrace his destiny. The symbolism of the sea journey and the treasure has been instructively analyzed by Kim Malville:

> These stories of descent into deep waters may be read as allegorical representations of the individualization of man. These are the life-renewing and life-restructuring acts which are exclusively available to the human individual.
>
> The creation myths involving the symbolism of earth-divers are elaborations on this theme of renewal through contact with the energies which lie deep within the individual. The myths involve creatures who dive into the water and reemerge, dripping with primordial slime but bearing remarkable treasures.[9]

Diving into the water, being swallowed by the whale, are symbolic of a return to the womb, where one bathes in the primordial, baptismal waters and resurfaces or is reborn to the light of a brighter sun, to a more clearly illuminated universe. If one is prepared for it, contact with the hitherto unutilized energies of life is a breathtaking world-transfiguration, for it leads to greater awareness of unconscious contents, and hence to a more complete picture of the psyche and its role in projecting the images of the world. In the following lyrics, Jimi Hendrix describes precisely such a baptismal experience in purifying waters, which effects a regeneration of the substantial body into the sublime spirit-body of *dharmakaya*, far removed from the physical and psychical dissonance of the mundane temporal world:

> *Hurrah, I awake from yesterday*
> *Alive, but the war is here to stay*
> *So my love, Catherina and me*
> *Decide to take our last walk*
> *Through the noise to the sea*
> *Not to die but to be reborn*
> *Away from lands so battered and torn*
> *Forever...*[10]

The Hindu myth of the churning of the cosmic ocean of milk serves to elucidate these ideas, seamlessly synthesizing them into a single, powerful image. According to the legend, at the beginning of creation the gods and demons worked together to churn the primordial ocean for the nectar of immortality (*amrit*). They used a mountain called Mandara as a churning rod, and twined the cosmic serpent Vasuki around it as a churning rope. The gods pulled the serpent from one side, the demons from the other, and after many years of tireless effort from both sides the churning began to yield results. One of the first products, however, was a terrible poison which threatened to destroy the world; Shiva once again came to the rescue by swallowing the noxious brew and thereby saving the earth.[11] Many other wonders and heavenly creatures issued forth from the ocean, until finally the *amrit* was obtained. The gods and demons then fought over possession of the *amrit*, until eventually the gods were victorious.

It may be recalled that the serpent represents the unlimited store of latent energy inherent within every person. When the serpent lies dormant, the energy remains stagnant, but when the serpent awakens and rises through the *chakras*, the energy is put to work in the task of reaching Nirvana.

So, if we attempt to decipher the mythological symbolisms using this knowledge, we can now translate the figure of the serpent in the churning myth as dormant cosmic energy, Mount Mandara as the *axis mundi* (central axis of the world, and our selves), and the primordial ocean as the unconscious. We thus arrive at the following formulation: by utilizing the vast reserves of primordial energy lying untapped and unused within ourselves, and putting it to the task of centering the self within the infinite expanse of the unconscious, the nectar of immortality is ours for the taking and the result will be a lifting of the illusory veil, a rebirth to our higher selves, independent of the ephemeral body. However, the poisonous, dangerous aspect (the *makara*) of the unconscious must never be neglected, and only a supreme yogi (which Shiva embodied) can consume the burning poison with impunity. The churning and the heroic adventure involve the same deep ocean, and so the dangers and fruits of the toil are also the same.

Footnotes

1. Don Henley, *The Heart of the Matter*.
2. Joseph Campbell, *The Hero with a Thousand Faces*.
3. The shadows can be understood as the projections of hyperbodies discussed earlier (see Chapter 3, under the heading *The Higher Dimension*).
4. The Who, *Anyway, Anyhow, Anywhere*.
5. The Rolling Stones, *Ruby Tuesday*.
6. In Joseph Campbell's terminology, this is the *threshold guardian*. In the Biblical story of The Fall, the cherubim with the flaming sword is the threshold guardian.
7. David Bowie, *Width Of A Circle*.
8. The Rolling Stones, *Wild Horses*.
9. Kim Malville, *Explorations in Science and Myth*.
10. Jimi Hendrix, *1983...(A Merman I Should Turn To Be)*.
11. The swallowing of the poison caused Shiva's throat to turn blue, and therefore he is also known as *nilkantha*, or "the blue-throated one." Recall in this connection the myth recounted in the previous chapter, where also Shiva saved the earth by receiving the shattering impact of the Ganges in his hair. Here again Shiva serves as a protector of the created world against a destructive aspect of the unconscious.

CHAPTER 10

THE STRUGGLE AND THE RETURN

The Mother Archetype

We now turn to another interpretation of the struggle of the hero, proposed by Erich Neumann in his book *The Origins and History of Consciousness*. In this book Neumann offers an interesting variation in analysis of the symbolism of the mythic hero adventure, which he uses to detail the stages of development in human consciousness and its struggle for independence from the unconscious.

In Neumann's schema, in the early stages of human existence man lived almost exclusively in the realm of the unconscious, and had an almost non-existent ego (sense of self), or differentiated consciousness.[1] The ego was contained only in germinal form in the original state of unconscious life. Its great struggle to break free from the ruthless grip of the unconscious was like a tiny satellite struggling to escape the gravitational pull of an enormous planet. For Neumann, it is this struggle which is portrayed in the mythological symbolism of the hero and the dragon, with the hero representing ego/consciousness, striving for freedom and autonomy, and the dragon representing the unconscious, trying to devour the hero and bring consciousness back into the fold of unconsciousness. Freud also recognized this aspect of the mythic scenario, and identified the ego as "the hero alike of every day-dream and of every story".[2]

With the evolving of the human race, consciousness gradually be-came stronger, more developed, until finally it was able to achieve inde-pendence from the unconscious. Each individual's ego also passes through the same stages of development. The newborn child exists in the same state of unconsciousness as did the earliest man. The child's progression to a state of awareness of its independent existence, and the further strengthening of its rational conscious faculties, is thus par-alleled in the history of the species *Homo sapiens*, and traces the same path of progress. Weak, insubstantial, and totally contained in the un-conscious as a germ, of potentiality at first, consciousness slowly in-creases in strength, struggles against the immense power of the uncon-scious and finally slays the dragon, emerging independent and guided by its own will.

With this much said about the struggle between consciousness and the unconscious, as detailed by Neumann, we are now ready to dis-cuss an extremely important and significant assertion made by him. He states that the figure of the Mother in mythology is to be understood as representing the unconscious. As the nascent consciousness is at first totally contained within the unconscious, so too every human being is initially contained within the mother's body, and therefore the mother is identified with the nourishing and all-encompassing womb of the unconscious. In the passage below, Neumann depicts the early state of consciousness, when it is still in a germinal state within the uncon-scious, the Great Mother:

> Doing nothing, lying inert in the unconscious, merely being there in the inexhaustible twilit world, all needs effortlessly supplied by the great nourisher — such is that early, beatific state. All the positive maternal traits are in evidence at this stage, when the ego is still em-bryonic and has no activity of its own.[3]

The Tao Te Ching has the following to say about the original state of the universe, before creation, which applies equally to the original state of unconscious existence before the ego's first stirrings to life:

> There was something undifferentiated and yet complete, which existed before heaven and earth.

Soundless and formless, it depends on nothing and does not change.
It operates everywhere and is free from danger. It may be considered the mother of
the universe.
I do not know its name; I call it Tao.

Here again the original, undifferentiated state of the unconscious is likened to a mother. The figure of the Great Mother, then, reveals itself to be a projection onto consciousness of the unconscious' archetype of itself.

As consciousness gradually grows stronger, it is no longer content to remain passive and dependent within the unconscious, and determines to free itself. The unconscious does not, however, easily relinquish its control; it attempts to subdue the newly aggressive ego and thus maintain its dominance over it. The mother archetype now reveals its dark and destructive aspect — the Terrible Mother, who would destroy and devour her son rather than grant him the independence for which he is struggling. Dragons, gorgons, sirens, and other mythical beasts that threaten the hero are variations of the Terrible Mother image, which must be overcome if consciousness is to survive on its own. Therefore, all depictions of heroes fighting against the mother, in her various terrible forms, essentially portray the unceasing struggle of the ego and consciousness against the consuming, devouring unconscious.[4]

Pink Floyd's song *Mother* is about precisely such an ominous and oppressive mother-figure, who maintains a vice-like grip on her son and employs any means at her disposal to keep him completely dependent on her:

Mama's going to make all of your nightmares come true
Mama's going to put all of her fears into you
Mama's going to keep you right here, under her wing
She won't let you fly, but might let you sing.

She is an extremely domineering and obsessive figure, who would emasculate and terrify her son to keep him helpless and dependent on her, in a state of perpetual infancy. The son becomes a tragic figure, for he has not succeeded in overcoming the mother and reaching maturity, i.e., consciousness has failed in its struggle and the individual has regressed to a primitive mental state.

Bob Dylan's *Isis*

Bob Dylan's song *Isis*, from his 1975 album *Desire*, is rich in mythic and psychological imagery, and deals with a hero journey and struggle against the archetypal Mother. In the song, the protagonist undertakes a perilous journey to a transmogrified Egyptian landscape, where he journeys through blizzards and snowstorms to reach a land where the pyramids are embedded in ice. The song is narrated in a bardic, storytelling format, and central to the story is the character of Isis, the ancient Egyptian goddess. Here, Isis is to be understood as a projection of the archetypal Great Mother, of the unconscious. The song begins:

> I married Isis on the fifth day of May
> But I could not hold on to her very long
> So I cut off my hair and I rode straight away
> For the wild unknown country
> Where I could not go wrong.

The protagonist/hero attempts to tame and dominate the Great Mother (i.e. the unconscious) by marrying her (with the patriarchal assumption that the wife is yielding and submissive in marriage), but fails in his attempt. He cuts off his hair, an apparent reference to the Biblical legend of Samson, whose strength lay in his hair — which was cut off due to deception by Delilah, another projection of the primal mother archetype. In Neumann's analysis, the attainment and increasing autonomy of higher consciousness, which has separated successfully to some extent from the encompassing unconscious, is often represented as the creation of the world. It is represented by symbols of light, the sun, the eye and the head. In this context, events such as cutting the hero's hair (which is associated with the head), blinding (consider Oedipus' self-maiming), driving the hero mad, and other calamities that befall him by the power of the Terrible Mother, symbolize failure to break the tenacious grip of the unconscious; they represent the dissolution of consciousness and its regression back into the original, formless, primordial state.

The hero then heads off to the "wild, unknown country," since he has failed in his current attempt and must find other, untried and uncertain means to escape from the relentless onslaught of unconscious drives and instincts. This is, in fact, the situation that confronts modern man: he is breaking free from the unconscious world of primitive man, and entering into hitherto unexplored territory, full of perils and the unimaginable terrors of isolation from the universal source of psychic energy.

The second verse of the song begins:

I came to a high place of darkness and light
The dividing line ran through the center of town.

The protagonist was, up to this point, still in the domain of the unconscious mind, in which all pairs of opposites, such as darkness and light, exist together in their original unity. However, the dividing line has been drawn which splits the polarities apart, and the struggle has begun. The separation of the dark and the light,[5] of Heaven and Earth, is a common motif in creation myths, and symbolizes the creation of the world of shapes and forms out of the formless void, the perceptual tearing asunder of opposites that previously were seen as defining and complementing each other. The world is now seen as described by Rudyard Kipling:

Oh, East is East, and West is West, and never the twain shall meet.[6]

In psychological terms, this represents the emergence of waking consciousness and ego from the dark night of the unconscious. The hero now embarks upon the perilous adventure which will transform him by forging and strengthening his weak and insubstantial ego, a process which has been taking place in the human race since it first crawled out of the primordial slime.

In the song, the hero is unsuccessful in his quest for buried treasure, resigns himself to his fate and prepares to return to Isis, signifying that she has triumphed and that he is prepared to sacrifice his hard won independence from her and disintegrate back into the abyss of the primordial night. However, when he sees her again, he has a change of heart and his resolve for independence is reawakened:

She was there in the meadow
Where the creek used to rise
Blinded by sleep
And in need of a bed
I came in from the east
With the sun in my eyes
I cursed her one time and I rode on ahead.

He rejects the hypnotic allure of Isis and pursues the goal of the attainment of his highest self, where he can experience the infinite scope of the universe in his waking, conscious state as opposed to experiencing it in the dark passivity of the unconscious, as in the primitive state.

Therefore, being overcome by sleep and exhaustion represents inertia and surrender to Isis, which the hero rejects by cursing her and moving on. He has the sun in his eyes, the eye representing the waking conscious state, and the sun representing the highest state which this consciousness can achieve. Conscious realization of contents and complexes deep within the unconscious is a process that, in everyday usage, is also referred to as "eye opening" and "mind expanding." Carried to the furthest possible extreme, this opening and expansion result in the eye, i.e. individual consciousness, being identified with the sun, i.e. universal or cosmic consciousness, as in the imagery of the Bhagavad Gita:

If the light of a thousand suns suddenly arose in the sky, that splendor might be compared to the radiance of the Supreme Spirit.

Even though he has left Isis behind and forged an independent path, the hero knows the daunting task ahead and the enduring, fatal attraction of the Eternal Feminine. In the closing verse of *Isis* he laments,

Isis, oh Isis, you mystical child
What drives me to you, is what drives me insane
I still can remember the way that you smiled
On the fifth day of May, in the drizzling rain.

This is reminiscent of the plight of Odysseus, who realized that he would have to be physically restrained (by being tied to the mast of his ship) in order to prevent his being destroyed by the seductive, maddening allure of the Sirens' song. In the words of Neumann:

> Since the dissolution of personality and individual consciousness pertains to the sphere of the Mother Goddess, insanity is an ever-recurrent symptom of possession by her or by her representatives. For — and in this lies her magical and fearful power — the youth burns with desire even when threatened with death . . .[7]

So, the heroic adventure comes to an end. However, with all that has been said about the ego's struggle for freedom from the unconscious, the overarching truth must always be borne in mind: the ego's victory is Pyrrhic unless it is accompanied by a recognition that the greater freedom of movement which is won is to be used to continually extend the field of consciousness by integrating ever larger portions of the unconscious into it, until the individual mind has become the Universal Mind. The *ground* of all the ego's activity is always the unconscious, which, when all superfluity has been removed, is the only ultimate reality. The liberated ego is like the soaring eagle, which is the very embodiment of absolute freedom but which could not exist without the infinite sky which forms the background to all its activity, and the air which supports its wings and lifts it high above the earth. As Dylan said, elsewhere:

My friends from the prison, they ask unto me
"How good, how good does it feel to be free?"
And I answer them most mysteriously
"Are birds free from the chains of the skyway?"[8]

If the victory of consciousness is used to expand it and open it up to the realization of unconscious forces and archetypes by creative and liberating endeavor, then the best of all psychic worlds is achieved. Ego and consciousness then enable the individual to go beyond the unconscious somnolence of the primitive by gaining enough psychic strength to slay the dragon, and yet retain a symbiotic relationship to his or her creative and self-regenerating center, the Good Mother in her benign and beneficent aspect. This is summed up in Jung's brilliant formulation:

> Fear of self-sacrifice lurks deep in every ego, and this fear is often only the precariously controlled demand of the unconscious forces to burst out in full strength. No one who strives for selfhood (individuation) is spared this dangerous passage, for that which is feared also belongs to the wholeness of the self — the sub-human, or supra-human, world of psychic "dominants" from which the ego originally emancipated itself with enormous effort, and then only partially, for the sake of a more or less illusory freedom. This liberation is certainly a very necessary and very heroic undertaking, but it represents nothing final: it is merely the creation of a subject, who, in order to find fulfillment, has still to be confronted by an object. This, at first sight, would appear to be the world, which is swelled out with projections for this very purpose... But nature herself does not allow this paradisal state of innocence to continue forever. There are, and always have been, those who cannot help but see that the world and its experiences are in the nature of a symbol, and that it really reflects something that lies hidden in the subject himself, in his own transubjective reality.[9]

Like all the great poets and bards before him, Bob Dylan tapped into hidden psychic reserves of the mind, and attempted to recount in the language of symbolism and imagery the heroic adventure of consciousness.

Return to the Worldly Plane

After undergoing the rigors and ordeals of the fantastic adventure, the world-redeemer returns, illuminated and radiant, to the world of everyday life that he had renounced in his quest for the truth. He has recovered the diamond of divine knowledge that was hidden deep in the subterranean bowels of the unconscious, and has been transmuted beyond recognition, from an ordinary mortal living an ordinary life to a Bodhisattva, a seer of prophetic stature. He could easily have forsaken the rest of humanity toiling in its misery, and remained aloof in the regions of sheer joy within the soul, self-content in his own bliss, but he chooses to return to the world of ordinary mortals, defiled as it is by the passions of the flesh, and of which Hamlet lamented: " 'tis an unweeded garden, that grows to seed; things rank and gross in nature possess it merely."

The savior returns out of his love for mankind, to redeem it and deliver it from the darkness that envelops it, and the whole of creation now sings the praises of the glorious hero-redeemer who has realized the divinity within himself and whose soul-matter has risen from the lower world of gross substance and united with the universal energy center and life force.[10] Of such a person, The Beatles said:

> *The wind is low*
> *The birds will sing*
> *That you are part of everything.*[11]

Thus, the transformed hero returns from his voyage into undiscovered expanses of the mind, his nerves and senses abuzz with the thrill of the mystical adventure. However, he now encounters a new, great dilemma. When he tries to communicate his experiences, insights, and newly-found wisdom to those around him, he cannot find the right words or expressions to convey the nature of the reality he has unearthed, for the simple reason that such words and expressions do not exist. He is faced with the problem put forth in the Svetasvatara Upanishad: "With whom shall we compare him whose glory is the entire universe?"

Since language is a product of the rational mind, it is impossible to describe spiritual and mystical revelations using ordinary language and concepts. The Spirit that exists behind the eye and the ear is ineffable and incommunicable. The Kena Upanishad has this to say about it:

> There the eye goes not, nor words, nor mind. We know not, we cannot understand, how he can be explained: He is above the known and he is above the unknown.

The Tao Te Ching concurs:

> *The Tao that can be told of is not the eternal Tao.*
> *The name that can be named is not the eternal name.*

Trying to find the right words and names for that which is impossible to pin down and label or categorize is like trying to grasp with one's hands the shadow of a flying bird as it moves on the ground, or like attempting to hold the ocean in a measuring cup. In the lyrics below, The Beatles speak of how the creative process is able to take these minuscule sections of the composite whole and turn them into abstract expressions that provide a hint of the universal totality which contains them.

> *Words are flowing out like endless rain into a paper cup*
> *They slither wildly as they slip away across the universe*
>
>
> *Thoughts meander like a restless wind inside a letterbox*
> *They tumble blindly as they make their way across the universe.*[12]

What remains in the paper cup is but a negligible portion of the gushing torrent, and broken fragments of the overall picture are the best that can be achieved within the constraints of human perceptual and cognitive limitations. So, realizing that it is impossible to directly communicate the nature of the highest truth, the prophet describes it as best he can — abstractly and indirectly, using the inner language of symbols and mythic imagery. The most he can do is to point the direction towards the truth and then leave it to those who are capable of following his directions to take up the journey for themselves. The prophets and saviors can only guide us, and warn us of the dangers and pitfalls on the way; they cannot grab us by the scruff of the neck, as a cat does with her kittens, and deposit us there.

After the symbols and guides have been proclaimed by the chosen ones, it is the task of the rest of society to correctly understand the hidden meaning behind them, and to not misinterpret them literally as though they were ends in themselves. The symbols are the boats that take us to the other shore, and once the far shore is reached the boat has outlived its usefulness. In fact it becomes a positive hindrance, for if one refuses to leave the boat and set foot on the soil of the unconscious, then the Self is doomed to remain an undiscovered continent. The people, places, and events related by the returned hero, therefore, are not to be mistaken for flesh-and-blood historical personages or actual tracts of land in the physical landscape, but as cosmic metaphors for forces and psychic factors extant in every human being. In practical terms, this is where the answer lies. The symbols in dream and myth speak to us of the timeless mystery and the suprapersonal forces at play within us. It is all very well to critically and rationally analyze these symbols and images, but in doing so we diminish their power and ability to effect a transformation within us. Bob Dylan sings:

> At dawn my lover comes to me
> And tells me of her dreams
> With no attempts to shovel the glimpse
> Into the ditch of what each one means
> At times I think there are no words
> But these to tell what's true.[13]

Myths, dreams, and fantasies are the only means at our disposal to talk about the ineffable power which cannot be reduced to the terms and concepts of language and thought. To allow the latent energy of the eternal symbols fully exercise their affective potential on us, we need to simply give them free reign in the mind, without any attempt on our part to analyze or classify them. Once they are absorbed and suf-fused throughout the psyche, they will of themselves work their al-chemy within us, transforming the base matter of our deluded minds into the pure gold of the highest illumination. In this context, it is use-ful to note what Heinrich Zimmer writes in regard to the true appre-ciation of Hindu mythology:

> The aim of the doctrines of Hindu philosophy and of the training in yoga practice is to transcend the limits of individualized conscious-ness. The mythical tales are meant to convey the wisdom of the phi-losophers and to exhibit in a popular, pictorial form the experiences or results of yoga. Appealing directly to intuition and imagination, they are accessible to all as an interpretation of existence. They are not explicitly commented upon and elucidated. . .

> They are effective primarily on a subconscious level, touching intui-tion, feeling, and imagination. Their details impress themselves on the memory, soak down, and shape the deeper stratifications of the psy-che. When brooded upon, their significant episodes are capable of revealing various shades of meaning, according to the experiences and life-needs of the individual.

> The myths and symbols of India resist intellectualization and reduc-tion to fixed significations. Such treatment would only sterilize them of their magic.[14]

This is why works of art and stories of old often strike an inner chord and leave us profoundly moved, without our even knowing why. They activate an archetypal or repressed image which had up till then been submerged in the recesses of the mind, but which is now "triggered" and irrupts into the waking, conscious state.

In principle, this is how the koans of Zen Buddhism are also to be understood. On the surface level of intellection and logic, such ques-tions as "What is the sound of one hand clapping?" and statements such as "This staff is not a staff and yet it is a staff" sound absurd, nonsensical, and hopelessly paradoxical. However, their function is not to elicit an answer but to lead to a realization. To fully understand them one has to lay aside the mind's peripheral layers of logic and abstraction,[15] and so let the koan penetrate to the deeper, visceral part of the self where it is *experienced affectively* with the whole being, not just beheld as an object for analysis by the intellect. By following the path of the koan one is led to an illogical absurdity, a dead end where the intellect must lay down its arms and admit defeat. The intellect must then be cast aside to let the koan through to the unconscious, where it unites with the supernal Self, and both koan and Self are then seen to be one. D. T. Suzuki writes:

> When the master tells the disciples to "think" with the lower part of the body,[16] he means that the koan is to be taken down to the unconscious and not to the conscious field of consciousness. The koan is to "sink" into the whole being and not stop at the periphery. Literally, this makes no sense, which goes without saying. But when we realize that the bottom of the unconscious where the koan sinks is where even the alaya-vijnana, "the all-conserving consciousness,"[17] cannot hold it, we see that the koan is no more in the field of intellection, it is thoroughly identified with one's Self. The koan is now beyond all the limits of psychology.[18]

And so, having returned from the fantastic adventure, the savior, out of his benevolence and love for mankind, offers mankind a path to salvation, a map to the treasure located within its heart. The road is a long and difficult one, but by following the path of our higher nature, and taking guidance from those who have walked the thorny path before us, we arrive safely at our destination. In the song *Are You Experienced?*, Jimi Hendrix says:

If you can just get your mind together
Then come on across to me
We'll hold hands and then we'll watch the sun rise
From the bottom of the sea.

The imagery is compelling. The experienced soul-master offers his hand in protection to the apprehensive and fearful traveler still gazing timorously along the open road. They then descend together to the nether regions of the unconscious (the sea) and there watch the sun rise, which is symbolic of a new dawn, a rebirth into pure consciousness. The sun represents this higher consciousness, and it is here that the imagery of the song reveals its true meaning: the attainment of universal consciousness by discovering the depths of one's own unconscious, surviving the experience, and seeing a glorious new dawn of the soul.

Footnotes

1. The discussion and characterization of consciousness and the unconscious in the preceding pages and chapters should be kept in mind for the discussion that follows. To recapitulate briefly, the ego and consciousness are responsible for the sense of a "self" that is separate from the world, and comprise the rational, analytical, and critical faculties of the mind. The unconscious is the deep, primal layer within the mind that is common to all, in which all opposites and dualities dissolve together into a monistic unity, and which is timeless, uncreated, and eternal.

2. S. Freud, *Creative Writers and Day-Dreaming.*

3. Erich Neumann, *The Origins and History of Consciousness.*

4. It should be noted here that victory against the Terrible Mother does not imply a destruction of the unconscious, or complete severance from it, for that is plainly not possible. Victory in this sense denotes the achievement of independence necessary for a well-developed and self-sufficient consciousness. This consciousness, although independent, needs to maintain contact and harmony with the forces of the unconscious, and any attempt at a total banishment of it will only lead to disastrous consequences, such as psychic inflation. The unconscious, in its Great Mother aspect, is the eternal nourisher and protector, and is indispensable for an integrated and well-adjusted personality.

5. See Illustration 8.

6. Rudyard Kipling, *The Ballad of East and West.*

7. Neumann, *The Origins and History of Consciousness.*

8. Bob Dylan, *Ballad in Plain D.*

9. C. G. Jung, *Psychological Commentary on "The Tibetan Book of the Dead."*

10. This force is called *prana* in Hinduism, and *ch'i* in Chinese philosophy.

11. The Beatles, *Dear Prudence.*

12. The Beatles, *Across The Universe.*

13. Bob Dylan, *Gates of Eden.*

14. Heinrich Zimmer, *Myths and Symbols in Indian Art and Civilization.*

15. One has to reach a state where, in the words of Jefferson Airplane's *White Rabbit*, "logic and proportion have fallen sloppy dead."

16. Suzuki identifies the upper part of the body, the head and eyes, with consciousness and intellection, and the lower part of the body, the abdomen and belly, with instincts and the unconscious. This meaning has been preserved in certain forms of speech, and even today one speaks of a "gut feeling" as an intuition that cannot be explained rationally or logically.

17. [Footnote in the original]: See *The Lankavatra Sutra* (London, Routledge, 1932), pp. 38, 40, 49, etc., and also my *Essays in Zen Buddhism*, Series 3 (London, Rider, 1951), p. 134.

18. Erich Fromm, D. T. Suzuki, and Richard de Martino, *Zen Buddhism and Psychoanalysis.*

CONCLUSION

The consciousness of modern man has evolved from its original state to such an extent that it constantly runs the danger of being cut off from its creative foundation in the primordial, collective unconscious. It is the function of art, religion, ritual, and myth to reconnect humanity to this infinite expanse within itself, and it does this in the language of symbols, imagery, and metaphor. Even though the struggle for increasing consciousness and freedom from the destructive aspect of the unconscious is imperative, and has proven to be so in human history, this can only be accomplished by an ever-increasing knowledge of the unconscious, and by being continually enriched by its vital, creative energy. It must not be regarded as a mortal foe to be annihilated and destroyed. The same unconscious that devours is also the source of inspiration and insight. It is the foundation and core of the self, and possesses infinite reserves of energy that lie waiting to be tapped and channeled towards the task of self-realization.

D. T. Suzuki gives the example[1] of the Zen master who trains in the art of swordsmanship. All his training and practice go into building up formidable skill and dexterity in his chosen art, but the final step in the training is the letting go of the self, reaching a state of "no-mind." At

this point, consciousness relinquishes its hold on the mind and the unconscious takes over, with its immense power of insight and even ex-
tra-sensory intuition. In addition, the unconscious now has at its disposal all the speed and skill that have been attained through training
and discipline. All the master needs to do now is to let his mind flow
freely, unimpeded by the intrusions of the conscious mind, not even
thinking of himself or the opponent. The sword moves as if by itself,
guided by the unconscious, which avails itself of all the technical skills
of mind and body that were acquired consciously. This is what distin-
guishes the true Zen master from the merely technically proficient — a
perfect example of consciousness and the unconscious blending together in life and in art, in perfect harmony.

This recalls the scene in the movie *Star Wars* where the young Luke
Skywalker is being trained in the art the light-saber[2] by Obi-Wan
Kenobi, his guru. Luke is practicing against a Remote (a robotic ball
used for combat training), which is bobbing and weaving in the air,
darting towards him unpredictably. He is unable to prevent it from
penetrating his defenses despite his fullest concentration, and just as he
is about to give up in frustration, Obi-Wan tells him to put on a blast
shield (a full face mask that completely covers the eyes), to let go his
conscious self, and to act on instinct. Since the eyes can deceive, it is
better not to trust them, and instead to reach out with the feelings, i.e.
the unconscious. With the blast shield in place, and acting purely by
intuition, Luke is finally successful in blocking the Remote with his
light-saber. When he tells his teacher that he could feel the presence of
a higher force operating through him when he had the blast shield on,
Obi-Wan tells him that he has taken his first step into a larger world,
beyond the confines of his empirical and verifiable experience. Luke is
on his way to understanding the meaning of the lines from the Tao Te
Ching:

> The five colors cause one's eyes to be blind.
> The five tones cause one's ears to be deaf.
> ... For this reason the sage is concerned with the belly[3] and not the eyes.

Today the eyes are dominant, and not the "belly." Objective observation of external facts has gained ascendancy over the subjective ex-

perience of internal ones. The active, aggressive *yang* rules over the quiet, yielding *yin*. From the standpoint of consciousness, the unconscious really offers very little in the way of practical value, and so it has been dismissed out of hand as nothing but a curious relic, an anachronism. What we have then is "egotheism," a ruthless cult of ego, and we are enslaved today under the tyranny of consciousness, which is after all just one psychic function among many. Instincts, feelings, and creativity, the other crucial facets of psychic functioning, have been left to atrophy and, unless they regain their rightful place, the moral and psychological health of society will continue their present freefall into oblivion. In the lyrics below, Peter Gabriel speaks of the pressing need to restore the instinctual, archaic portion of the psyche to equal footing with the discriminating, differentiating, and categorizing mind:

> *And all my instincts, they return*
> *And the grand facade, so soon will burn*
> *Without a noise, without my pride*
> *I reach out from the inside.*[4]

Once the instinctual energies (or libido, to use Freud's term) and archetypal symbols are given their due, the external world collapses like a house of cards; one's hubris disintegrates, and the inner world is seen in its all-expansive form. This is, however, perhaps too lofty an ideal to aim for, since the vast majority of people enter this world and leave it with hardly a glimpse of the universe within, which is in fact the determinant of the universe without. How many Buddhas, Christs, and Lao-Tzus has human history offered up? Realistically, the best that can be hoped for on a large scale is that people achieve a relatively harmonious balance between the various contending forces within their beings. Alas, this more conservative hope also looks to be over-optimistic.

With the present laser-like focus on rational consciousness, and with the corresponding devaluation of the unconscious, the risk looms large of an undesirable and unpredictable reaction formation or *enantiodromia* to redress the grievous imbalance. The unconscious does not accept meekly its relegation to secondary status. The further down one

tries to push the unconscious, the more intense and primitive its com-
pensatory reactions become. The archaic and primordial instincts,
which are harmless in the daylight, fester in the fetid depths, and there
assume a barbarous, malignant, and wholly destructive form. Renouncing the unconscious is equivalent to renouncing the vast, unseen portion of the self that contains imprints and patterns from earliest history. Only by reconciling the past with the present is the necessary
equilibrium maintained for a hopeful future. The following lyrics by
Bob Marley have never been more poignant or relevant than they are
today:

> In this great future
> You can't forget your past.[5]

The past has, sad to say, been forgotten and denied, and is now exacting payment of arrears. Thus, while the twentieth century saw the
greatest advances (mainly by Western civilization) that the world has
ever seen, in science and weaponry, it was also the most savage and
bloody in human history, and saw an unprecedented number of wars,
genocides, and mass exterminations. Very few of the wars were initiated for convincing and justifiable political, social, or economic reasons.
They simply resulted from the wild flailing of the caged, unseen creature within, lashing out in delirious rage at being cast down and ig-
nored. Until the unconscious is accepted, affirmed, and embraced, it
will show its most terrifying face and the most sophisticated and
lethally efficient of weapons will continue to be in the hands of this
berserk, infuriated beast. Mankind will then once and for all enter the
belly of the whale.

At the heart of the crisis is the fact that modern man's art and mythology have failed to keep pace with his increasing rationalizing capacity and technical achievements. Jung has said that man reconciles
the outer world of objects with the internal world of archetypes and
unconscious images through symbols, whose function it is to transfer
energy from one realm to the other. Mankind's advances have certainly
not been matched by a corresponding set of symbols to help the new
homo sapiens to cope with the new external reality, and so even though

man has charted the movements of the planets down to the last detail and has plotted the precise motions of subatomic particles, he remains unlettered in the ways of his inmost being, and his psychic energy is finding ever more destructive outlets for its release.

The symbols of religion and mythology, to which the large mass of the people in the world today cling as irrefutable fact, come from a world of the remote past, and many of them need to be updated and reformulated to address the technocentric, machine-dependent world of the present. The machines that man has created have transformed the conditions of human existence, but the inner world of spirit and self has been allowed to stagnate and decay. This is because the modern worldview sees man as having been cast out from paradise and flung down to an alien and hostile world below which, rather than being an extension of his psyche, represents a bitter enemy. Hence, man finds himself in an interminable battle against the "outside," against nature and other human beings, and it is to assist in this great battle that he has developed his technology. His devices and machines help him subdue nature, and his weapons of destruction, torture, and slavery help him control and dominate other men.

The person of today has severed the umbilical cord that ties him to Mother Nature. This is necessary if he is to develop as an independent, free and self-guided being; but he has not taken the next crucial step of engaging in creative, productive activity and inquiry which will allow him to work free from constraints while still being spiritually and morally replenished from his inner *sanctum sanctorum*. This searching for one's undefiled nature and self, while going about the task of living with eyes fully open, is a constant process of birth and renewal, without which there is only discontentment and pathological alienation. As Erich Fromm explains:

> When we speak of birth we usually refer to the act of physiological birth, which takes place for the human infant about nine months after conception. But in many ways the significance of this birth is overrated. In important aspects, the life of the infant one week after birth is more like intra-uterine existence than like the existence of an adult man or woman. There is, however, a unique aspect of birth: the umbilical cord is severed, and the infant begins his first activity:

229

breathing. Any severance of primary ties, from there on, is possible only to the extent to which this severance is accompanied by genuine activity.[6]

Part of this activity is the unearthing of images and symbols deep in the collective psyche, and this particular activity has long been the realm of bards and poets, and other artists, to which list the modern era has added psychologists, filmmakers, and a whole host of others. The true visionaries of popular music have provided contemporary interpretations of universal ideas and themes, and presented them to an audience larger than the seers of antiquity could have imagined. It is now the task of the audience to sift the grain from the chaff, to differentiate between art of true creative expression and that of shallow market-oriented packaging, and to allow the inspirational power of genuine creativity to reconnect the audience to its innermost self. Jung writes the following about the function of art in culture and society:

> It is constantly at work educating the spirit of the age, conjuring up the forms in which the age is most lacking. The unsatisfied yearning of the artist reaches back to the primordial image in the unconscious which is best fitted to compensate the inadequacy and one-sidedness of the present. The artist seizes on this image, and in raising it from deepest unconsciousness he brings it into relation with conscious values, thereby transforming it until it can be accepted by the minds of his contemporaries according to their powers.[7]

David Bowie captures the same spirit wonderfully when he says of the true artist (in this particular case, Bob Dylan):

> *You sat behind a million pair of eyes*
> *And told them how they saw.*[8]

Bowie recognized it as the artist's essential function to re-discover the lost symbols and modes of expressions of the creative life, and to offer his insight to the less pioneering and gifted of his contemporaries.

Freud, with his more narrowly defined and literal-minded approach to things, proposed that art is a reconciliation between the pleasure-principle and the reality-principle. The artist at first gives his creativity full rein to explore the unconscious via wishes and fantasies, and then returns to reality with the knowledge that his explorations have given him. Freud says:

> An artist is originally a man who turns away from reality because he cannot come to terms with the renunciation of instinctual satisfaction which it at first demands, and who allows his erotic and ambitious wishes full play in the life of phantasy. He finds the way back to reality, however, from this world of phantasy, by making use of special gifts to mould his phantasies into truths of a new kind, which are valued by men as precious reflections of reality.[9]

Consider the imagery employed by Bob Dylan (whom Bowie held to be a model of the inspired and inspirational artist), when he talks about imparting the truths to which his artistic temperament has afforded him uncommon access:

> *And I'll tell it and think it and speak it and breathe it*
> *And reflect it from the mountain so all souls can see it.*[10]

The rupture of the vital link to the unconscious, the creative bedrock of the human soul, has resulted in psychic and social disorders on a large scale, and humanity, with all of its scientific progress, needs to rediscover this link or risk an even greater and more violent widening of the schism. The disorientation and displacement that are the result of this isolation from the creative core of humanity is described by Bob Dylan:

> *How does it feel?*
> *To be on your own*
> *With no direction home*
> *Like a complete unknown*
> *Like a rolling stone.*[11]

Like a rolling stone that gathers no moss, the isolated personality has no roots in the subsoil of the psyche, the self, to give him/her stability, and no sense of kinship or mutual bonds with others. This leads inevitably to a sense of desolation and emptiness. Music has enormous potential to restore balance and harmony on a large scale, and to act as a healing balm to the wounded soul of modern man. However, this potential remains to be fully realized. The way out of the tangled highways of time and space seems to have been lost irretrievably, but the route is only obscured by wind-blown debris, it has not been eliminated. It must be the unrelenting effort of the artist to remove this layer of dust and detritus, and show us the way once again. Music in its highest form has the power to tap into undiscovered depths of the soul, and from those depths to exhume hidden psychic contents that can now serve as beacons to light our way.

Sri Aurobindo has compared the act of artistic creation with that of the creation of manifest forms and shapes out of the unmanifest Self. Just as the artist brings forth ideas and content that are fundamentally contained within his inmost being, so the world is simply the self-manifestation of the Eternal principle. Sri Aurobindo writes:

> Existence that acts and creates by the power and from the pure delight of its conscious being is the reality that we are, the self of all our modes and moods, the cause, object and goal of all our doing, becoming and creating. As the poet, artist or musician when he creates does really nothing but develop some potentiality in his unmanifested self into a form of manifestation and as the thinker, statesman, mechanist only bring out into a shape of things that which lay hidden in themselves, was themselves, is still themselves when it is cast into form, so is it with the world and the Eternal. All creation or becoming is nothing but this self-manifestation.[12]

If anyone doubts that symbols and images have a vital function in providing an outlet for inner, unexpressed mystical intuitions, he/she need only look at the back of the U.S. dollar bill, at the engravings of the obverse and reverse of the Great Seal of the United States, which was designed by the founders of the American Republic over two hundred years ago.[13] The obverse of the seal shows an American bald eagle which clutches in its left talons a bunch of arrows, and in its right talons a laurel spray. These may be said to represent the unification of war and peace within solar consciousness (the eagle). Furthermore, the bird holds in its beak a scroll bearing the inscription *E Pluribus Unum*, "Out of the many, one." This can be read as an allusion to the containment of the *saguna* world of diverse forms in the underlying formless *nirguna* field.

The reverse of the Great Seal shows a pyramid with the date 1776 printed in Roman numerals on the base. At the summit of the pyramid is an open eye, radiating an effulgent light. The scroll on the bottom of the seal bears the inscription *Novus Ordo Seclorum*, "A new order of the ages." The date on the base of the pyramid represents the temporal world, confined to a specific moment or age, and the eye at the summit is the blazing eye of Eternity, corresponding to the mystical third eye of Shiva. When this third eye is opened and directed outwards it emits a fiery glow that consumes all the worlds, but if it is directed inwards it produces the supreme insight of the Infinite Self.

This mystical inner eye of spiritual vision is the one that needs to be opened if one is to awaken from the slumber of ignorance and apprehend the supernal light that shines within each human body and radiates outwards to combine with all the other similar effusions to form one universal glow. In the Bhagavad Gita, Krishna briefly confers the vision of the Divine third eye onto Arjuna, who then stands shaken to the depths when he beholds for the first time Krishna's universal form. Contained in this form Arjuna sees all the gods and all the beings of creation, and the splendor of infinite beauty which illumines the whole universe. When Krishna resumes his mortal, human form he tells Arjuna that he has just seen the supreme and most exalted vision that is denied even to the highest gods in heaven. This is the true meaning of the mystical symbols on the back of the dollar bill that millions of people exchange every day, unaware of the ancient mysteries that they carry around in their wallets, which in fact speak directly of a new order of the ages and of heightened consciousness.

What shape this new order takes is yet to be made clear, for everything depends on which human priorities and tendencies are attended to by the times, and which are suppressed. Every person harbors within him/herself, within his/her unconscious, infinite potential for greatness, wickedness, courage, selfishness, love and hate; the extent to which these are inhibited or encouraged depends on each individual, and on his reactions to the influence of society. The degree of liberation from social conditioning that a person achieves, and the intensity of his passion for harmony and relatedness with others, ultimately dictate the path that he will choose. Each of us harbors within us the tyrant, the saint, the artist, the deviant, and the hero. Which of these asserts themselves as dominant within the individual varies from person to person. Fromm writes:

> Man, in any culture, has all the potentialities; he is the archaic man, the beast of prey, the cannibal, the idolater, and he is the being with the capacity for reason, for love, for justice. The content of the unconscious, then, is neither the good, nor the evil, the rational nor the irrational; it is both; it is all that is human. The unconscious is the whole man — minus that part of man which corresponds to his society. Consciousness represents social man, the accidental limitations set by the historical situation into which an individual is thrown. Unconsciousness represents universal man, the whole man, rooted in the Cosmos; it represents the plant in him, the animal in him, the spirit in him; it represents his past down to the dawn of human existence, and it represents his future to the day when man will have become fully human, and when nature will be humanized as man will be "naturalized."[14]

By focusing exclusively on the ego and thus allowing himself to be manipulated and deceived by society, man dissociates himself from the infinite possibilities that lie before him; he limits himself to the conditions and circumstances particular not only to the human situation, but even more narrowly to the situation of his specific history and society. He becomes bound to the parochial, and is removed from the universal. In the song *Quicksand*, Bowie sings:

> I'm not a prophet or a stone-age man
> Just a mortal with the potential of a Superman
> I'm living on
> I'm tethered to the logic of Homo sapiens
> Can't take my eyes from the great salvation
> Of bullshit faith.

Each person has the potential to be constantly in the process of enlarging and widening his/her consciousness, to break free from the restraining harness of physical and mental limitations. The majority fail to do so because of their own mental and creative inertia or, more commonly, because of the overpowering influence of restrictive and divisive social structures and institutions. First, it is necessary to muster the energy and will to revolutionize one's consciousness and attain enlightenment, and then to work to help others to achieve the same internal revolution, so that the role of society can then be made nurturing and life affirming, rather than oppressive and life thwarting.

The way forward, if humanity is to avoid being destroyed by internecine conflicts, lies in recognizing the universal soul of humanity, and in breaking down the psychological barriers that obscure and distort this fundamental fact. In the words of Erich Neumann:

> The collective unconscious of mankind must be experienced and apprehended by the consciousness of mankind as the ground common to all men. Not until the differentiation into races, nations, tribes, and groups has, by a process of integration, been resolved in a new synthesis, will the danger of recurrent invasions from the unconscious be averted. A future humanity will then realize the center, which the individual personality today experiences as his own self-center, to be one with humanity's self.[15]

This sentiment is echoed by Bob Marley in the joyous proclamation below, which shows that the inner voice that has spoken to the gifted ones over the ages has forever said the same thing:

One love, One heart
Let's get together and feel alright.[16]

Footnotes

1. In: Erich Fromm, D. T. Suzuki, and Richard de Martino, *Zen Buddhism and Psychoanalysis.*
2. A type of sword, which uses an energy blade instead of a metal one.
3. That is, the instincts. See Chapter 10, footnote 16.
4. Peter Gabriel, *In Your Eyes.*
5. Bob Marley, *No Woman No Cry.*
6. Erich Fromm, D. T. Suzuki, and Richard de Martino, *Zen Buddhism and Psychoanalysis.*
7. C. G. Jung, *The Spirit in Man, Art, and Literature.*
8. David Bowie, *Song for Bob Dylan.*
9. S. Freud, *Formulations on Two Principles of Mental Functioning.*
10. Bob Dylan, *A Hard Rain's A-Gonna Fall.*
11. Bob Dylan, *Like a Rolling Stone.*
12. Sri Aurobindo, *The Life Divine.*
13. See Illustration 9.
14. Erich Fromm, D. T. Suzuki, and Richard de Martino, *Zen Buddhism and Psychoanalysis.*
15. Erich Neumann, *The Origins and History of Consciousness.*
16. Bob Marley, *One love/People get ready.*

APPENDIX

In Illustration 10, I have attempted to show pictorially the main themes, concepts, and processes that are discussed in the book. This appendix will deal only with the mystical and psychological aspects that are discussed, for the musical correspondences to these ideas have already been dealt with in the main text. It is my purpose here to condense as much as possible of the information in the preceding discussions into a single diagram, and to use it to clarify the salient points of the ideas presented.

The dashed arrows represent processes or forms of dynamic activity, whose nature will be discussed below. The solid arrows are simply for labeling purposes.

At the highest level, the diagram depicts the relationship of individual to universal consciousness. The large central circle represents the Universal Self, which is also called variously the collective unconscious, *dharmakaya*, and the Supreme, subtle spirit of life. This is the realm of the *nirguna* world, without attributes or properties, in which all opposites exist together in an undifferentiated harmonious unity. At the center of this circle I have marked Brahman, which symbolizes the eternal, timeless, and formless essence of the entire universe. This is the universal energy center which pervades all life and matter, and provides the energy for all processes and actions everywhere. Each and every

237

form of life derives its nourishment and sustenance from this ever-replenishing source; it emerges from this source at the beginning of life, it takes sustenance from it during its brief tenure, and it returns into it at the close of its temporal existence.

The four smaller circles A, B, C, and D in the diagram, located around the central one, represent the individual self as it has been variously conceived. Since each circle represents a different model of the same individual self, Circles A, B, C, and D can be viewed as different planes of a single three-dimensional sphere that represents the individual self in all its various forms. They have only been separated into different circles here on paper because of the limits of drawing in two-dimensional space. In working within these limitations, the four smaller circles can be visualized best as being superimposed on top of each other, such that what is explicitly labeled in one circle can be thought of as being implicitly labeled in the others.

Circle A represents the Western religious and scientific view of the self as a split-off, dissociated entity, isolated from the rest of the world. For this reason, the circle has been drawn with no point of contact with any of the others. Similarly, the horizontal line within the circle is the dividing line separating consciousness, or ego, from the personal unconscious of the individual, and this separation is ordinarily felt as the distinction between intellect and instinct, reason and emotion. The average person believes the boundaries of his body (the circumference of the smaller circles) to be the definitive demarcation between himself and the external world, and considers that within this body his independent self is contained. His ordinary perception, therefore, is of himself as irreconcilably detached from the world and his fellow man, and from this jutting promontory he views others as similarly isolated centers of localized consciousness.

According to the mystic or Eastern perspective, however, these smaller circles and their boundaries represent the false sense of ego and identity under which the mass of humanity is laboring, and which is the root cause of all its suffering. I have shown this mode of experience in the diagram with the dashed bi-directional arrow marked *Ordinary Perception (Maya)*. In this view, the tendency to see others and the self as dissociated egos is pure illusion, or *Maya*, and has to be overcome if knowledge is to prevail over *avidya*. The boundaries of the circles and the lines within them are thus to be understood as merely tenuous membranes that must be punctured by the yogi so that the contents of all the circles flow together and mingle inseparably. The mystics would seek to collapse all the smaller circles so that they dissolve into the Universal Self and only the large central circle remains. In the case of the infant and the primitive, these small circles are so negligible as to be just tiny dots on the surface of the large sphere, which is why they both exist in a state of perpetual *participation mystique* with the world and are close to the supreme Divinity.

In the mystical approach, Atman, the individual soul (as marked in Circle D), is to be identified with Brahman, the Universal Soul, and the movement towards this identification is indicated by the dashed arrow marked *Enlightenment*. This movement entails a shifting of the center of gravity from the solitary ego to the suprapersonal center of the psyche, a translation of focus from the localized to the infinite. The ego and personal contents of the mind (represented by Circle A) are discarded, and the Atman moves to joyful dissolution into Brahman, all dualities and conflicts falling by the wayside. This upward, liberating movement is that of the rising kundalini energy, and so the dashed arrow is divided into the seven fiery centers of energy, the *chakras* (with the two central dots at the beginning and end of the arrow representing the lowest and highest *chakras*, respectively). The lowest *chakra* is that of existence wholly within the unenlightened self, split off from the rest of humanity, and the highest *chakra* is that of indissoluble union with the Universal, all-expansive self. The inward hero journey also follows the direction of this arrow, from the temporal, space-delimited body to the secret depths of mystical rapture within the heart of all hearts.

Therefore, in the mystical *weltanschauung*, the only reality is the large central circle, the Universal Self. All the smaller illusory spheres of circumscribed individual consciousness are really grounded in the larger one, which is why Circle D has been drawn so as to be in contact with it. In actual fact, there is *only* the transcendent One, without beginning, without end, eternal and unchanging, and everything else is just trickery and deceit. However, this is clearly impossible to encapsulate in a diagram[1] or in words, and it can only be fully understood when it is thoroughly experienced as an intimate truth. The diagram can merely indicate an arrow moving two points together, but as to what this merging means emotionally and psychically, no lines and words can ever convey. The proof of the pudding is entirely in the tasting.

If one were to attempt to describe the Western Judeo-Christian ethos using this diagram, the first step would be to move all the smaller circles away from the central one so that they are not touching at any point (like circles A and B). The central one would now be labeled *God*, and the smaller ones labeled *God's Children* or *God's Creations*. A new dashed arrow would have to be drawn from the small circles to the big one — it could be labeled *Prayer* or *Supplication*; and another arrow could be drawn going the other direction, labeled *Blessing* or *Judgment*. The circumferences of all the circles would, in this case, be understood as hard and unyielding. This is in essence the religious view of the West — God and man separated by an unbridgeable rupture, and only able to communicate with each other through the channels of worship, in the one direction, and Divine will, in the other. God, the strict but loving father, listens to the entreaties of His children and takes note of their transgressions, and when the hour is at hand, He passes final judgment on them. As a caveat we should add, here, that many Christian and Western mystics have had a strong affinity with the Eastern minds, but their thought is by no means dominant, or even well represented, in the prevailing attitude of the Occident.

We now turn our attention to the psychological concepts presented in the diagram. Circle B illustrates the Freudian view of the mind. This view is based solidly on Western rationalism and so this circle, like Circle A, is disconnected from all the others, and all psychic processes are shown as being internal to the individual self. According to this model, consciousness and the (personal) unconscious are separated by a filtering layer, which regulates the manner in which psychic contents pass from one zone to the other. Unpleasant or socially tabooed thoughts and impulses are pushed down from consciousness into the unconscious, where they form the vast complex of repressed memories and impulses. These repressions are now actively maintained by the selective filter, which actively expends energy to perform its task. Often there is a let up in this energy, during sleep, for instance, so that the repressed contents slip through to consciousness — but not before being modified by *dream-distortion*, the active agent of which is called the *dream work*[2]. The material in its unmodified form, as it exists in the unconscious, is called the *latent dream thought*, and the dream as it is remembered upon waking, after having being subjected to the dream work, is called the *manifest dream*. The dream-work performs its function of transforming the latent dream thought to the manifest dream by a number of methods, such as condensing the repressed latent thoughts together, displacing their psychical emphasis, and a whole host of other mechanisms too involved to enter into here.[3]

Circle C, along with its associated interactions, renders the essential features of Jungian analytical psychology that are covered in this book. The thickened crust covering consciousness is the *persona*, or *personae*, that is, the various faces or masks that a person shows to the exterior world and which hide his true, inner personality. Once this facade is stripped off, we come to consciousness and the personal unconscious, which are essentially the same as they were envisioned by Freud. However, going even deeper, we come to the collective unconscious, which Jung himself identified with the Universal Self, or *dharmakaya*, of Eastern philosophy, and which has therefore been marked as such in the diagram. This is why Circle C, like Circle D, is grounded in the large central circle. In synthesizing this notion of the *persona* with mystical thought, it is interesting to consider an idea set forth in Hinduism, and elaborated by a number of Western commentators such as Alan Watts, Joseph Campbell, and Heinrich Zimmer. According to this idea, the universe is regarded not as a series of chance happenings and accidental interactions between an untold number of discrete, insignificant, individual souls, but instead as an immense and exuberant cosmic drama, a finely scripted play (*lila*). In this universal drama, however, there is but one Actor, Brahman, who is playing all the parts, and who puts on a different mask, or *persona*, to play the role of each transient individual. Peel away any given mask and there is Brahman behind it. Jung himself hinted at this meaning when he said that the *persona* is a mask of the collective, rather than the personal, self. He wrote:

It [the persona] is, as its name implies, only a mask of the collective psyche, a mask that feigns individuality, making others and oneself believe that one is an individual, whereas one is simply acting a role through which the collective psyche speaks.[4]

A person's feeling of being only this one particular self and not any other is due to the Actor's total absorption in playing this, and every other, part.

It was Jung's recognition of this deepest and most fundamental core of being that afforded him such insight and understanding of Eastern thought; and Freud's repudiation of it explains his complete aversion to all forms of occult or mystical phenomena. Freud looked to the personal unconscious, to the events, acquaintances, and proclivities peculiar to an individual, to elucidate the hidden meaning behind all dreams.[5] Jung, on the other hand, looked to the collective unconscious for the source of all transpersonal and universal themes that appeared in individual expression. Thus, he treated myths and art as a sort of universal dreams, whose recurrent motifs often appear in individual dreams and creative outpourings as well.

Furthermore, Jung rejected Freud's concepts of dream distortion and dream work, as well as the idea that there was some active agent that was modifying the contents of the psyche so as to deceive the conscious mind. For Jung, the abstract and abstruse character of symbols was to be attributed to the fact that they were expressing something beyond the capacity of the human mind to contemplate in its totality. That being the case, metaphors and analogies were the only means to refer to it, and were not the results of deliberate obfuscation by some trickster within the mind.

The collective unconscious, then, is common to all humanity and life, and within it lie embedded the eternal archetypes, the inherited patterns of behavior and perception accumulated within the human psyche since the time life began on earth. These archetypes are too vast and deeply ingrained to be experienced directly, and so they are projected onto consciousness via the constellated symbols of dream, myth, and religion. This I have shown in the diagram with the arrow labeled *Projection*, which passes through the portion marked *Symbols* before it reaches consciousness. Therefore, it can be seen that consciousness receives images and ideas not only from the personal unconscious, but also from the collective unconscious, all of which are crystallized into symbols before they reach us in the normal waking state.

This illustration is at best an extremely rough outline of the most prominent features of Eastern and Western thought; but perhaps it can be used as a basic conceptual framework within which the myriad details can be arranged and organized — much as symbols are used, whatever a person's background.

Footnotes

1. Perhaps the best illustration of this idea would be an empty sheet of paper with no lines or markings on it.

2. Labeled in the diagram as *Distortion*.

3. The interested reader is referred to Freud's monumental work *The Interpretation of Dreams*, or, for a more readable and concise account, to his *On Dreams*.

4. C. G. Jung, *Two Essays on Analytical Psychology*. This subtler and deeper meaning can be arrived at in the diagram by tracing a path from the *persona*, through the interface to the Universal Self, to the center, which is Brahman.

5. It is for this reason that I have drawn no process (dashed) arrows between the *Universal Self/Collective Unconscious* and Circles A and B, for these two circles represent the Freudian and dualistic world view, which place no value in such scientifically unprovable and mystical concepts as an all-suffusing cosmic consciousness, and reject them out of hand.

In the same collection from Algora Publishing:

Time & Ego. Judeo-Christian Egotheism and the Anglo-Saxon Industrial Revolution
— by Claudiu A. Secara

A Passion for Democracy: Benjamin Constant
— by Tzvetan Todorov

The Tyranny of Pleasure
— by Jean-Claude Guillebaud

Coping with Freedom: Reflections on Ephemeral Happiness
— by Chantal Thomas

Refounding the World: A Western Testament
— by Jean-Claude Guillebaud

Death and Life
— by Paul Fairfield